WONDERS OF MAN

FLORENCE

by Francis King

Photographs by Nicolas Sapieha

NEWSWEEK, New York

NEWSWEEK BOOK DIVISION

Edwin D. Bayrd, Jr.   *Editorial Director*
Mary Ann Joulwan   *Art Director*
Laurie P. Winfrey   *Picture Editor*
Eva Galan   *Assistant Editor*
Diane Raines Keim   *Picture Researcher*

Alvin Garfin   *Publisher*
William Urban   *General Manager*

WONDERS OF MAN

Milton Gendel   *Consulting Editor*

ENDSHEETS: *Giotto's designs for the campanile of the Duomo called for multicolored marble panels inset with bas-reliefs by Luca della Robbia and Andrea Pisano. Most of the bas-reliefs have been replaced by copies, but the soft pastel revetments survive intact.*

TITLE PAGE: *So vividly did the most popular of English novelists describe the western prospect of the Arno as seen from the covered walkway of the Ponte Vecchio that it has been known ever since as the "Dickens View." It is rarely photographed—and rarely more lovely than at sunrise, when the day's first sun floods the worn paving stones of the bridge.*

OPPOSITE: *In heraldry, both the lion and the lily are symbols of Florence—an apt pairing for a city of commerce and culture, a once bellicose city-state turned to gentler pursuits. Donatello has combined both symbols in his statue* Marzocco, *executed around 1420.*

Library of Congress Cataloging in Publication Data

King, Francis Henry.
Florence.

(Wonders of man)
Bibliography: p.
Includes index.

1. Florence (Italy)—History.   2. Florence
(Italy) in literature.   I. Sapieha, Nicolas.
II. Title.   III. Series.
DG736.K56   945'.51   81-81993
ISBN 0-88225-308-5   AACR2

Printed and bound in Japan

Contents

Introduction

If Florence can be said to have a sister city, that city is almost certainly Kyoto. Like Japan's ancient capital, Florence is a city with a past so glorious it cannot help but overshadow the present. Both former capitals have surrendered their commercial and cultural preeminence; both, like the best pearls, grow dimmer but more lustrous with age. What was once raw vitality is now restrained gesture. Where once one encountered the white heat of artistic creativity one now finds the warm glow of treasures preserved. In the crucible of the fourteenth and fifteenth centuries, Florentines forged the High Renaissance—Dante and Boccaccio in literature, Brunelleschi and Michelangelo in monumental sculpture and the monuments that housed them, Giotto and Fra Angelico in painting, the Platonic Academy in philosophy. This was the city's golden age, an epoch in which Florence produced great merchant princes as well as great princes of the church. Many of these princes, both temporal and spiritual, were members of the extraordinary Medici family, whose fortunes and those of their native city were inextricably joined for generations. The long decline that followed the Age of the Medici is a golden afterglow—the tawny light of Tuscany reflected off the Arno, which snakes through the city's center, and off the buildings that rise near the river's banks. These include such justly famous structures as the Duomo, sheathed in polychrome marble and surmounted by Brunelleschi's mighty dome; the Palazzo Vecchio, with its overhanging battlements and rugged walls, a sturdy testament to the power of the city's merchant oligarchs; the Ponte Vecchio, whose covered span once housed goldsmiths' shops; Santa Maria Novella, with its luminous interiors by Andrea and Bernardo Orcagina; Santa Croce, embellished by Giotto's frescoes and Fra Angelica's paintings; and the city's major museums, the Uffizi and the Pitti. No catalog of the treasures to be found in Florence can adequately reflect the richness of its patrimony—so great that it spills out into every public square and crops up around every corner—for in a very real sense all Florence is a museum, a vast open-air archive that is an enduring expression of the greatest cultural efflorescence in all of human history.

THE EDITORS

FLORENCE IN HISTORY

FIORENZA

I

The City of Flowers

Guidebooks and tourist brochures often refer to Florence—Florentia to the Romans, Fiorenza in medieval times, Firenze today—as "The City of Flowers" or "The Flower City," but the derivation of the city's name is far from certain. Some people ascribe it to the flower-filled fields where the Romans marked out their new town; others, to the fact that they did so during the annual *Ludi Florales*, a festival honoring the goddess Flora, protectress of the blossom. Another theory holds that Florentia was a corruption of Fluentia—a reference to the flowing waters of the Arno. In Latin, *florens* means "flourishing," so it may also be that the name was given solely for reasons of luck, just as we now have our Cape of Good Hope, our Fairhavens, and our Concords.

At all events, Florence is indeed a city of flowers. In the spring especially, they are to be found not merely in every garden and courtyard and on every surrounding hill but also piled up for sale all over the city. In the years immediately after World War II, tiny, unpressurized planes used to hop and skim between Florence and such cities as Milan, Rome, and Naples, and it was then possible to peer down into the innumerable gardens that, from the ground, are either totally invisible behind high walls or else barely visible through wrought-iron grilles and gates. From any vantage, however, Florence and its environs give an immediate impression of natural fertility. This is a fertility that has been carefully husbanded over the centuries, to ensure that the vines and olive trees fundamental to the agriculture of the region flourish on terraces only a few yards beyond the urban sprawl (and even within it). Such

care also ensures that such flower markets as the one held between five and seven in the morning in the Piazzale degli Uffizi display every species of flower from simple bunches of daffodils to branches of the white, waxen lilies so often imitated in church silverwork and so often carried by the Angel of the Annunciation in the art of the region.

Florence is a City of Flowers, a "flourishing" site, in a metaphorical as well as a literal sense, for its cultural efflorescence is one that few cities of the world have ever paralleled. What is even more remarkable is that so many of its treasures, the products of this extraordinary cultural flowering, are not shut away in museums or enclosed behind walls and railings but are everywhere accessible. At each step, the beauty of the past goes with you—even if the noise and ugliness of the present unfortunately go with you too. The whole city is a kind of vast open-air museum; but whereas the word "museum" suggests something frozen in the perfection of death, Florence is vividly alive, with precisely the same kind of people—volatile, ardent, contentious, quick-witted, inventive—who once jostled the poet Dante Alighieri or gaped at his lovely Beatrice.

Just as, today, the Acropolis best evokes the whole history of Athens and the Capitol the whole history of Rome, so the Piazza della Signoria performs a similiar service for Florence. Many of the approaches to the great square are streets so tall and narrow that one has a feeling of claustrophobia walking up their dimness and dankness—and then a feeling of liberation as one comes out into the space and brilliance of the Piazza. It is easy to see this

change as symbolic of the emergence of Florence from the artistic and intellectual constriction of medieval times into the freedom of the Renaissance.

Dominating the Piazza, as indeed it dominates the whole of Florence, is the looming bulk of the Palazzo Vecchio—or the Palazzo dei Priori, as it was originally called. At once strong and graceful, it too seems symbolic of an historical transition: its strength, as of a fortress, was necessary in a city where dissension within once posed quite as many dangers as attack from without; its elegance was desirable in a city that was, at the time the Palazzo Vecchio was erected in the thirteenth century, already setting itself the classical ideal not merely of *mens sana in corpore sano* but of both *mens* and *corpus* at perfect ease in surroundings ideally fitted for them. With such a building in it, no one could call the Piazza della Signoria "the drawing-room of Europe," as the Piazza San Marco in Venice has often been called. The Piazza della Signoria is splendid, dignified, and commanding, but it does not smile, it does not invite; "the assembly-hall of Europe" would be a more appropriate title.

The construction of the Palazzo Vecchio, with its overhanging battlements and rugged walls four stories high, the last of these thrust out and supported by arches set on brackets of stone, was instituted in 1299 for the *priori*, or priors, collectively known as the Signoria, who had become the rulers of Florence. It is therefore the concrete symbol of the passing of power from the *grandi*, or nobles, to a merchant oligarchy. Like all those who find themselves newly in authority, the Signoria were eager to raise an edifice that would both proclaim their splendor and prove unassailable against any attempt to unseat them.

Tradition has it that the architect of the Palazzo Vecchio was Arnolfo di Cambio—although no written record of this exists—and that he was initially hampered in his plans by being forbidden to build on the site of a palace, recently razed, that had belonged to the hated Uberti family. At a time when Florence was riven by civil strife the Uberti represented the Ghibelline faction, allies of the Holy Roman Emperor who had been conducting an intermittent war with the Guelph faction, allies of the pope. Arnolfo pleaded, but his masters were adamant: where the traitors' nest had stood, there the sacred foundations of the house of the people could not be laid. Another site had to be chosen, an irregularly shaped adjacent plot, and the building that rose upon it may be rightly regarded as a monument to the Guelph victory in a struggle that had for so long consumed the city.

As so often happens when a great artist is faced with what at first seems to be a cruelly inhibiting problem, Arnolfo was stimulated to produce a masterpiece—superior among Florentine buildings even to his Duomo or Santa Croce. Far from detracting from its beauty, the irregularity of the site, and consequently of the building itself, merely accentuates it. The bell turret opens like a flower from a slender stem; resting on its great, cantilevered machicolations, it seems to hang there in miraculous defiance of the laws of gravity. Into the substructure of this tower, which is some 330 feet high, Arnolfo incor-

Florence at the beginning of the fourteenth century was a city riven by internal dissension and imperiled by external aggression. Weakened by a protracted civil war between "Black" and "White" factions, the once-mighty city-state was no match for its enemies in Rome or in Paris. In these dire times the citizenry needed a rallying point, a tangible symbol of their city's past and future greatness—and they found it in the Palazzo Vecchio (right), begun in 1299 and completed in 1314. As much fortress as palace, this severe Gothic structure bespoke the new municipal government's determination to withstand all attacks, from within or without. It was possible to survey the whole of Florence from the building's 308-foot-high bell tower, and it was possible to withstand any unruly mob behind its massive walls. In the photograph at left, the shadow of Michelangelo's legendary David *plays upon the honey-colored walls of the Palazzo Vecchio, just as it has for four centuries.*

porated an existing tower, called *La Vacca*, or "The Cow," that had once adjoined a palace built by the Foraboschi family. Bought by the municipality, that palace had been subsequently demolished, with only the tower surviving. The huge bell atop the new tower, cast by a Sienese named Lando di Pietro in 1322 and said at the time to be the largest in the world, would be tolled to summon citizens at times of danger or rejoicing. It was common on such occasions to say *La Vacca muggia*—"The cow is mooing." When, in 1530, the Florentine Republic was overthrown, this bell was flung down and smashed in an act of symbolic vandalism.

In 1349 a wide stone platform, called the Ringhiera, was erected in front of the northern façade of the Palazzo, as though to acknowledge that the rulers of the city, who had previously cooped themselves up inside for the two months of their period of office, need no longer treat the Palazzo like some beleaguered citadel. Henceforth they would harangue the people from the Ringhiera in a manner reminiscent of the fiery orators who delivered speeches from the Rostrum in the days of classical Rome. And it was from this vantage point, on May 23, 1498, that they would look on as "Savanarola's soul went out in fire"—to use the words the English poet Elizabeth Barrett Browning chose to describe the death by hanging of the renowned religious reformer. In 1812, an invading French army destroyed the original Ringhiera; the present Ringhiera is a small-scale reproduction of the original.

At the northern angle of the Ringhiera (see map, page 164) is a copy of Donatello's *Marzocco*. It was

executed between 1418 and 1420 and originally stood in Santa Maria Novella, where it wore a golden crown bearing an inscription by Franco Sacchetti:

Corona porta per la patria degna
A ciò che libertà ciascun mantegna
[I wear the crown for our deserving land,
That freedom is maintained on every hand.]

The name Marzocco, generally thought to be a corruption of Martocus, the diminutive of Mars, refers to the heraldic lion that appears on the shield of the Florence Commune and symbolized its power. Live lions were once kept near the Palazzo Vecchio, in the street called for that reason the Via dei Leoni, and the birth of a cub was always an occasion for rejoicing. The fourteenth-century chronicler Giovanni Villani tells the story of a lion that escaped from its cage, not in the Via dei Leoni but in the Piazza San Giovanni, and roamed through the streets. At Or San Michele it grabbed a small boy and held him in its paw. The mother, shrieking in terror, eventually succeeded in reclaiming her son, for the lion, behaving in a miraculously docile fashion, offered no resistance. The boy's father had recently been assassinated, and the general supposition was that the lion had spared the child so that he could grow up and exact vengeance for the crime—which, in time, he did. This anecdote is one of many which illustrate the superstitious reverence the Florentines had for these beasts, often interpreting the vagaries of their behavior as omens and portents.

At an angle of the walls of the Palazzo Vecchio there is a raised stone seat, just large enough for

17

Michelangelo, who resided in Florence during the first decades of the sixteenth century, left his adopted city a number of certified masterpieces—and, local legend has it, one genuine curiosity. The masterpieces include the David *that once stood in the Piazza della Signoria and the* Pietà *in the Duomo; the curiosity is the crude bas-relief seen at left. According to a durable but dubious folk tale, Michelangelo sketched a companion's profile on a wall of the Palazzo Vecchio while engaging the friend in conversation—and without once turning around to check the accuracy of his caricature, which the artist applied to a stone directly behind him. The likeness was deemed accurate—even if the story is not—and the lines of the sketch were later carved into the stone. Not far from this spot stands Baccio Bandinelli's* Hercules and Cacus (right). *The commission for this important work was supposed to go to Michelangelo, but Bandinelli, most envious of artists, schemed to obtain both the commission and the marble. Two Medici popes backed him, and Michelangelo's version of the heroic statue became one of history's great might-have-beens.*

two, where nowadays you will often see tourists flopping down to rest their feet, change the film in their cameras, or consult their guidebooks. On the rough surface of the masonry behind, the face of a man has been coarsely incised in low relief. According to Florentine tradition, this is the work of Michelangelo. He was leaning against the wall, a group of his cronies around him and a pencil in his hand, when he began surreptitiously to sketch the face of one of them—the pencil behind his back, so that he had no idea how the likeness was taking shape. Later, someone reverentially carved out the lines. The correctness of this attribution is as dubious as, say, that of Byron's signature on a column of the temple at Sunium; but the story, however apocryphal, is a pleasing one, for it shows how, even then, the Piazza was fulfilling one of its present-day functions, that of the open-air club.

If the Palazzo Vecchio represents a period of transition from feudalism to oligarchy and from war to peace, the magnificent arcade of the nearby Loggia dei Lanzi represents one of stability and calm. The mixture of round arches with Gothic design and ornament, so characteristic of buildings in Florence, has about it no suggestion of conflict or stress. Indeed, there is an assurance about the very openness of the structure to every comer. This arcade was originally called the Loggia dei Priori or the Loggia della Signoria, and it was only when Duke Cosimo I, son of Giovanni delle Bande Nere, stationed his German lancers in the nearby Via Lambertesca in the sixteenth century that it acquired its present name. Another earlier name for this perfect build-

ing—its *pietra serena* providing the same kind of contrast with the *pietra forte* of the Palazzo Vecchio as its airy elegance does with all that solid ruggedness—was the Loggia d'Orcagna, because of a belief, totally unfounded, that Andrea Orcagna, creator of the tabernacle of Or San Michele, had also been the architect of the Loggia.

As many a tourist soon learns to his surprise, rain is by no means uncommon in Florence, so that the original reason for building the Loggia was the same as that for building, in 1338, an earlier loggia in the rival city of Siena: to provide a covered space where public ceremonies could be conducted without any fear of the elements. Begun in 1374, with the kind of demolitions of ancient buildings that now arouse furious protests from conservationists, the Loggia was completed in 1382. Two years later a reception for the visiting Bishop of Ravenna was held there.

Since that time this arcade has fulfilled a variety of functions. It has been a place of ceremonial and a place of assignation. It has been a doss-house: less than half a century after its completion, Leon Battista Alberti, one of those universal men in whom the Renaissance was so rich, commented that its portico provided a refuge under which old men might pass the heat of the day. It has been a market, whether for flesh, for lottery tickets or, in the years immediately after World War II, for black-market cigarettes, sewn into the voluminous overcoats of the sellers. It has been a listening post: "Hundreds of men stand here for hours, as if they had nothing else to do, talking ceaselessly in deep Tuscan tones," the Victorian traveler Augustus Hare re-

corded. In 1961, the Queen of England, like the Bishop of Ravenna some six hundred years before her, received an official welcome there, looking patiently bemused as the city herald sang out verses in her honor. Above all, the Loggia is an outdoor sculpture museum of a kind rare at its inception but common enough today.

The finest work the Loggia contains is Benvenuto Cellini's *Perseus*, and a comparison between the critical reaction—a hundred years ago and today—to this bronze and to another, Donatello's *Judith with the Head of Holofernes*, which stands on the Ringhiera, provides a fascinating illustration of the vagaries of taste. In his guide of 1897, Grant Allen describes the *Perseus* as "one of the most perfect works of its kind cast in metal," adding that the *Judith* is "heavy and confused." Nowadays, the seesaw having tipped, connoisseurs tend to praise the latter work at the expense of the former.

Donatello's *Judith* was cast for the Medici in approximately 1460 and originally stood in the courtyard of the Palazzo Medici. Then, in 1495, when Piero II, known as the Unfortunate, was expelled from the city and his palace sacked, *Judith* was moved to the Piazza and, as a warning to such as the Medici who sought to establish an autocracy, an inscription was added: *Exemplum Salutis Publicae Posuerunt*—"The citizens set this up as an example of public safety." After it had stood for a time on the Ringhiera, near the same sculptor's *Marzocco*, the civic worthies decided that it was unseemly to display a statue of a woman who had decapitated a man. As a result *Judith* was moved a number of

21

With the possible exception of the Statue of Liberty, there is no more familiar or more frequently copied statue in all the world than Michelangelo's David. *Indeed, what modern visitors to Florence see in the Piazza della Signoria is a copy executed in 1873, the year Michelangelo's original was moved for safekeeping to the Galleria dell'Accademia, where it now stands not far from the* Four Slaves *intended for the tomb of Pope Julius II and left unfinished at the time of the great sculptor's death. What twentieth-century visitors to Florence like about* David—*that the figure seems at once larger than life and incredibly lifelike—is what sixteenth-century viewers most objected to. They felt that Michelangelo had flouted the classial conventions of masculine beauty, and in their rage they pelted the statue with stones when it was unveiled in 1504.*

times—until, in 1919, it returned to the Ringhiera, where, fittingly in this age of women's liberation, it remains on view today.

Like Pygmalion, Donatello was inspired by the life of his own work and, while working on the *Judith*, he would often stand back from it and cry out, "Speak! Speak!" What this bloodthirsty young woman might have said to him, had she responded to his plea, is an interesting speculation. Although sometimes criticized for the meagerness of its modeling and the restraint of its action—the latter no doubt due to Donatello's habit of confining his design within a compact space so that no outstretched limb ran the risk of damage—this statue was nonetheless innovative inasmuch as it was one of the first works of sculpture intended to be seen from a variety of positions, instead of merely from in front.

Cellini's *Perseus* was commissioned by Duke Cosimo I in 1553, after the Medicis' return to power. Cellini, who had impulsively left the service of Francis I of France in 1545, a decision he almost immediately regretted, has left us a vivid, if unduly self-congratulatory account, in his memoirs, of the difficulties involved in casting so vast and elaborate work—at one point he had to throw his own plate into the furnace for lack of any other source of bronze—and of the triumphant reception the work was finally accorded, with poets affixing laudatory verses to the pillars of the Loggia when *Perseus* was finally revealed to the public's astonished gaze. (From what one knows of Cellini, he might well have written the verses himself and then paid the poets to stick them up!) He also gives an amusing account, one that will

strike a sympathetic chord in every artist, of how Cosimo di Medici pressed him to name the price of his masterpiece, thus impaling him on the horns of a dilemma: whether to ask for a little, and so be sure of payment—or to ask for a lot, and risk getting nothing.

Some people claim to distinguish the bearded face of a man on the back of Perseus's helmet and assume that Cellini intended it to be a self-portrait. On the other hand, there is no question about the splendid statuette on the base of Cellini's work: the figure, as beautiful as that of Perseus himself, is of the youthful Hermes—and beneath, the Latin inscription, so apt for a creature so airy: *Ad astra volo*—"I fly to the stars." Cellini has depicted Hermes as Puck, about to put a girdle round the world.

Both Donatello's grim warrior-maid and Cellini's almost effeminately coquettish youth were intended as warnings. The former notified those who attacked the Republic that they were liable to lose their heads; the latter conveyed the same message to those who contemplated attacking the Medicis.

The best sculptor of Cellini's day was Giambologna, who had gone to Rome from Douai to study and then, having been adopted by a wealthy Florentine dilettante named Ecchietti, had made his patron's city his home. Tradition has it that, when he carved his *Rape of a Sabine*, which took its place in the Loggia near the *Perseus* in 1583, Giambologna was deliberately attempting to show that he could bring precisely the same virtuosity to the less tractable medium of marble that Cellini had brought to bronze. In any case it is a splendid, if overformal, performance, one foreshadowing the Baroque.

A decade later Giambologna was to create the superb equestrian statue of Duke Cosimo I that stands in the Piazza. He received the commission after Cosimo's death from the duke's son and heir, Ferdinand, who provided the sculptor with a special studio for the work in deference to its size and complexity. Since the history of Florence is literally multilayered, it is no surprise that the remains of a second-century A.D. Roman bath should have been found beneath the paving stones around this statue.

The other great work of sculpture outside the Palazzo Vecchio is Michelangelo's *David*. (What modern visitors see is a copy, executed in 1873, when the original was moved to the Accademia to protect it from chemical erosion.) This most famous of Florentine statues was commissioned by the Opera del Duomo—the Cathedral Works Office, subsidized by income from forests in the upper valley of the Arno—in 1501, and it was unveiled, to a mixture of enthusiasm and execration, in 1504. No doubt contemporary critics of the work, who for four days pelted it with stones, objected to the *David* on the same grounds as its modern critics: in his representation of this ferociously determined youth, Michelangelo deliberately flouted the Greek ideals of perfect proportion and perfect beauty. With his overlong limbs and overlarge head, hands, and feet, this *David*, in transition from adolescence to manhood, might well be some *contadino* that Michelangelo had seen—and that one sees today, a rural youth on a visit to Florence from, say, his father's Tuscan smallholding. Before *David*, it is difficult to think of any heroic statue of a comparable realism.

At the time the commission was granted an admirer of Michelangelo's named Piero Soderini was the *gonfalonier*, or leader, of the Republic of Florence. He no doubt saw *David*, intrepidly doing battle with the giant Philistine, as an accurate representation of Florence, defying its often larger and seemingly more powerful neighbors, and when the statue was set up, Soderini naturally went to view it. In general he expressed enthusiasm, but he did criticize the nose. Was it not too big? Michelangelo, picking up a chisel and hammer, climbed a ladder set against the statue and pretended to work on its nose, even letting some marble dust drift down from his pocket, where he had secreted it. Soderini was delighted: "Bravo! Bravo! Now you've really given it life!"

A Piazza statue group that is less generally admired is Bartolommeo Ammanati's *Fountain of Neptune*, completed in 1575. Ammanati, who was a protégé of Cosimo I's wife and of the artist and critic Giorgio Vasari, won the commission against the competition of Cellini, Vincenzo Danti, and Giambologna, then a young man. In time even the sculptor himself was to show a lack of enthusiasm for the fountain group, which Florentines scornfully named *Il Biancone*, freely translated as "the blancmange." (Ammanati has a better claim to artistic fame in the elegance and simplicity of his Arch of Symmetry, the Ponte Trinita, blown up by the Germans in 1944 but reproduced, perfect in every detail, in 1958.) Such was the lack of respect for this pudgy Neptune, presiding over the fountains like some out-of-condition swimmer, that the populace began to wash their linen in the water and to pollute it with their rubbish.

A notice, still visible today, was then put up on the Palazzo Vecchio, warning those who indulged in such practices that they would liable to a fine. Michelangelo himself was said to be unable to pass the statue without muttering, " Ammanati! Ammanati! What a beautiful statue you've messed up!"

In addition to the Palazzo Vecchio, the Loggia dei Lanzi, and a number of medieval houses, the Piazza also contains the Tribunale de Mercatanzia, or Merchants' Tribunal, inscribed upon its completion in 1358 with the motto *Omnis Sapientia a Domino Deo Est*—"All Wisdom Comes from the Lord God"; the small Palazzo Uguccione, erected in the 1550s; and the former Palazzo Landi, an unhappy nineteenth-century attempt to emulate the heyday of Florentine architecture. Thus, in a comparatively small area, buildings can be found that represent every phase of the city's history.

As political change occurred, so the Palazzo Vecchio underwent a parallel change of appearance, of use, or of both. For instance, when Gualiterro di Brienne, born in Greece of French and Asian blood, was sent to Florence in 1342 to quell the dissension between the Guelphs and Ghibellines, he hurriedly strengthened all the palazzo's defenses, even blocking the steps of the Ringhiera.

The huge Salone dei Cinquecento was built in 1495 for meetings of the Council of the Republic. Its *capo maestro*, Simone Cronaca, so called because of his long-windedness, was accorded the commission to design the council hall because he was a friend adherent of Girolamo Savanarola, then at the height of his power, and because he was a mechanical genius with an unsurpassed talent for moving weights and raising scaffolding. In 1523 the autocratic rule of Cosimo I displaced the republican Signoria—and the Palazzo became the Medici's principal residence. To celebrate the marriage of Cosimo's son Francesco I to Joanna of Austria, decorations were added to the Cortile in 1565 under the direction of Vasari; and it was Vasari who supervised the creation of the Studiolo of Francesco I.

After Cosimo I moved out of what had come to be called the Palazzo Ducale—and into the new Palazzo Pitti on the other side of the Arno—the name Palazzo Vecchio first came into use. The building then suffered a decline in importance and a consequent dilapidation, a course not reversed until the provisional governments of 1848 and 1859 used it as their assembly hall. During the brief period from 1861 to 1875, when Florence was the capital of a united Italy, the Chamber of Deputies and the Foreign Ministry were housed in the Palazzo Vecchio, today the seat of the municipal government.

The history of the Piazza and the Palazzo is, in miniature, a history of Florence itself, with its revolts, conspiracies, and factions, its passing of rule from nobles to a mercantile oligarchy, its hectic alternations between republicanism and autocracy, its long acquiescence to Medici domination, its brief emergence as a capital city, and its present role as a center of commerce and tourism. Similarly, the buildings and statuary that make up the Piazza represent, in miniature, a history of the most fruitful period of Florentine art. If one had only an hour to spend in Florence, no place could teach one more.

It is no accident that Florence is nicknamed "The City of Flowers."
Flora is the Roman goddess of flowers; florens, Latin for "flourishing";
and Florence abounds in flourishing blooms at practically every
time of the year. The city's principal flower market, held annually
in the predawn hours when most of the city is still asleep, offers
the buyer choices ranging from the mundane to the truly exotic. The
streets offer that same variety to the visitor, adding color at every turn.

II

Dark of Winter

Despite the increasing frequency of archaeological discoveries in recent years, the early history of Florence remains largely a matter of tradition and conjecture. Burial finds, often made inadvertently when a farmer has been turning over his land or a builder has been excavating fresh foundations, make clear that there were Stone Age dwellers in this area millennia ago. That there were dwellers on the site of Florence itself from the tenth century B.C. is attested by such finds as the graves, containing urns of a distinct Villanovan type, discovered when the medieval center of the city was destroyed to make room for the modern Piazza della Repubblica.

The earliest inhabitants about whom we possess more than faint glimmerings of knowledge are the Etruscans, who made their settlement not down in the valley of the Arno but on Fiesole, a hilltop above it. One of the earliest of Florentine chroniclers, Malespini, maintained that, long before the advent of the Etruscans, Noah's Ark had come to rest on the summit of Fiesole when the waters of the Flood subsided—making Florence the first city to be founded after the earth reemerged from the waters. In this more skeptical age, we may beg leave to doubt this and begin our history of Florence where doubting leaves off—with the Etruscans.

It is probable that the Etruscans came originally from Asia Minor. And although they may have come as conquerors and marauders, they soon settled down to the peaceful occupations of farming and trading. The site of Fiesole, on a commanding hill, and the cyclopean masonry that girds it, both indicate an armed domination; but the location was clearly not chosen for military reasons alone. Placed as it was between two ancient trade routes, Fiesole could control all commerce north from the ferry of the Arno and from Arezzo by way of Candeli.

Apart from the opportunities for trade, the Etruscans must also have been attracted by the region's suitability for forestry, farming, and mining. There were those hillsides all around Fiesole, at that period hardly touched or inhabited, with tall, solid trees that must have appealed at once to this maritime people, these builders of ships. And there was the fertile land, revealed when the trees had been felled. (In Etruscan legend, significantly, the god Tages rises up, in the form of a boy, from earth turned back by the plough.) And there was the Tuscan copper. There is ample evidence, from Bronze Age implements found in this area, that copper was being mined in the coastal marshlands long before the Etruscans arrived on the scene, but it was the Etruscans who gave this activity a new impulse—wanting quantities of the precious metal to use as barter for imports from the East.

Having established themselves securely in Fiesole, the Etruscans decided to found a colony down by the Arno. This is thought to have happened about 200 B.C., at a time when the Romans had already broken Etruscan military power and, having embarked on an extension of the Via Cassia to Arezzo, Florence, and Bologna, were becoming the guarantors of law and order in the district. Archaeological digs have revealed an Etruscan settlement to the east of modern Florence, in an area long since covered up by growing city's suburbs.

It is instructive to sit on the terrace of a café in modern Fiesole and attempt to imagine what an Etruscan arrival in 1000 B.C. would have seen from the same position. Today there can be in all the world few distant views of a city more beautiful, with the dome of the cathedral, the many towers, the occasional cypress tree showing above the rooftops—and across the valley the Tuscan commune of San Miniato with its eleventh-century cathedral and the line of hills behind it. Centuries of cultivation have produced an undulating softness on every side. But that Etruscan invader of three thousand years ago would have looked down on a less inviting scene of tangled, sparsely inhabited forests, with a far wider and more turbulent river fretting its way between them. He would, no doubt, have been glad for the fortifications upon the hill.

In 83 B.C. the Roman general Lucius Cornelius Sulla, backed by a devoted army and in possession of enormous treasures, many of them plundered from Mithridates, returned to Rome from Asia Minor and at once set about trying to wrest power from the hands of the *populares*—the party opposed to the senatorial nobility—who had seized it in his absence. By a grave miscalculation, the Etruscans, in a dream of regaining their former position of dominance, sided against Sulla. The general won, as he was wont to do, and to revenge himself on those cities that supported his opponents he confiscated their lands for distribution to his soldiers—and in some cases, even razed their buildings to the ground. Both these fates overtook Etruscan Florence, so that when, a few years later, a new city arose, it was an essentially Roman one and many of its inhabitants were army veterans.

But just as surely as the Etruscans gave their name to the district, Tuscany, of which Florence is the center, so they contributed much both to it and to the city. Dante wished wholeheartedly to believe that primitive Florence had been peopled by colonists from Rome—so much so that in the *Convito* he speaks of Florence as *la bellissima e famosissima figlia di Roma*—"the most beautiful and the most famous daughter of Rome"—but even he was obliged to confess that Etruria had played some part in her conception, through a mixture of barbarian blood with the *sementa santa*, or holy seed, of the Eternal City. To this "*confusione*" he ascribed many of the evils that befell his birthplace.

In contrast, the nineteenth-century English writer John Ruskin insists in his *Mornings in Florence* that most of the outstanding achievements of Italy can be in some measure ascribed to the Etruscans. Although their tangible legacy is a meager one of rock-hewn tombs, a few inscriptions, and some works of art of dubious beauty, their influence remains, if only in the ancient families—Adimari, Corsi, Pazzi, Guadagni, Strozzi—who came down to Florence from Fiesole and are popularly thought to be of Etruscan ancestry.

Despite the fact that Florence has no surviving Porta Augusta, as at Perugia, and no surviving Colosseum, as at Verona, the outline of the Roman city can be faintly discerned, as in a palimpsest, under the map of the later one. Excavations have shown that the Romans fixed the center of their city on the

site of what later became the Mercato Vecchio—and, still later, after extensive demolition, the Piazza della Repubblica. Here they built their Forum and their Capitol. In other parts of the present town, remains have been found of temples, baths, and walls. Street names like Via delle Terme (Street of the Baths) and Via Porte Rossa (Street of the Red Gate) are further reminders of Roman influence. So too, in more concrete form, are the Piazza Peruzzi and the Via Torta (Curved Street), which follow the arc of the long-vanished Roman amphitheater.

The Roman city was a small one, not much above a third of a mile square. To facilitate the journey of travelers on the Via Cassia who wished to get from the sparsely inhabited far bank of the Arno to Florentia itself, the Romans constructed a bridge, later known as the Ponte Vecchio. Like those Japanese temples that have been rebuilt after each fire or earthquake, always in precisely the same form, so the much-rebuilt Ponte Vecchio remains in essence the same and can, in a sense, be said to have survived until the present.

Since Florence played an inconspicuous part in the history of the Roman empire, it is difficult to cobble together any record of events. In A.D. 250, during the Christian persecutions under the emperor Decius, a Greek called Minias—later beatified as San Miniato—suffered martyrdom. The fact that he was not a native Florentine and that he alone seems to have met this fate suggests that most of the inhabitants of third-century Florence still followed what Dante called "the false and lying gods"—and that Christianity had few adherents in the region.

By the late fourth and early fifth centuries a dramatic change had taken place in this regard with the emergence of those three great scholar-saints, Ambrose, Jerome, and Augustine. All were profoundly steeped in classical learning, and by applying it to the elucidation of Christian doctrine they won over many people, both influential and humble, to the faith. Of this trio, Ambrose is the one most relevant to the history of Florence. As Bishop of Milan, he had the courage to reprove Emperor Theodosius for having ordered a wholesale massacre in the Greek city of Thessalonica, even exacting penance from him. At one point in his often stormy career, Ambrose had to flee Milan and take refuge in Florence. During this exile from his see, he not only dedicated the Church of San Lorenzo—the present San Lorenzo, begun by Filippo Brunelleschi, stands on the site of his old basilica—but also, in a typically inspired choice, consecrated as its bishop a man called Zenobius.

The story of the life of Zenobius is largely obscured by a perfumed mist of legend. For example, little credence can be given to those who still point out a tower in Via Por Santa Maria and declare that the holy man lived there with two of his disciples, Eugenius and Crescentius, both of whom, like Zenobius himself, were later beatified. Equally dubious is the story of how, when Radagasius and the Goths arrived at the gates of Florence in A.D. 405, Bishop Zenobius at once gave himself up to constant prayer. In particular he invoked Santa Reparata, whose festival, which falls on October 8, was then being celebrated. The intensity of his devotion, it is said, so impressed the saint that she appeared, the Florentine *giglio*, or lily, in her hand, and, despite the unsuitability of this weapon, soon put the invaders to rout. The grateful citizens at once erected a church in her honor—the present Duomo, or cathedral, stands approximately on its site—and so it is that this obscure Palestinian saint, martyred in the persecutions of Decius, has become closely associated with a city she never visited in life but is credited by legend with saving long after her death.

The more skeptical may prefer to ascribe Reparata's cult to the fact that the most influential Christians in fifth-century Florence came from Asia Minor and were therefore familiar with her life and martyrdom. (Significantly, many of the Christian tombstones dating from this era bear Greek, not Latin, inscriptions.) Those who regard Zenobius and Santa Reparata as the sole saviors of the city also overlook the less spiritual Stilicho, who, having freed Britain from the invasions of the Picts, Scots, and Saxons while acting as regent for the emperor Theodosius, withdrew his troops from what was regarded as an insignificant island to cope with the Gothic invasion of Italy. It may indeed be impossible to say who was chiefly responsible for the saving of the beleaguered city, but we do know that Zenobius made many converts as a result of it.

Radagasius might be expelled, but other German invaders, crashing down upon Italy in wave upon violent wave, would prove more determined—and more successful. In 476, the last Roman emperor of the West, Romulus Augustulus, was forced to abdicate his throne in favor of the barbarian Odacer.

Shortly thereafter the Ostrogoth chieftain Theodoric, an Arian Christian known both for admiring the philosopher Boethius and for having him brutally murdered on suspicion of treason, killed Odacer and seized the throne. Everywhere, now, civilization was in retreat. From his capital at Byzantium, Justinian, emperor of the East, was able, thanks to the exploits of his great general Belisarius, to rout the Gothic hordes and make Italy once again a part of his empire; but on his death on 565, political and economic chaos returned and the last vestiges of civil government began to disappear.

Innumerable single causes have been found for the disintegration of the Roman empire, from the spread of malaria to the spread of Christianity, from lead poisoning to soil exhaustion, from an overreliance on slaves to an overindulgence in hot baths. But the economic cause, if not the only one, is certainly the most important. Once imperialist expansion had reached its limits, a fundamentally agrarian economy, relying on horses and oxen for energy—surprisingly few water wheels or windmills existed—began to stagnate, with the inexorable consequences of a slump in population and a decline in living standards. From ignorance as much as negligence, the new rulers from beyond the Alps did nothing to revivify the old Roman tax and legal systems, so efficient in the heyday of the empire, or to improve the economic circumstances of their subjects. Public edifices fell into disrepair and were then plundered to provide the materials for building private hovels. Land that had been laboriously reclaimed over many centuries was allowed to sink back into unprofitable, mosquito-breeding marsh. Roads reverted to grassy tracks. In its combination of despairing anarchy and brutal tyranny, the situation was like that in much of Africa today.

In this period of unhappy retrogression, which lasted from the fifth to the eighth century, there was a continuous exodus from the towns into the country, and Florence, no exception to this tendency, was largely depopulated. There was little money to be made out of trade; sometimes it would not yield even a precarious livelihood. The great families withdrew to their castles, raised their own private armies, and made no contributions either to civic life or civic revenues. It was from this aristocracy and their serfs that the feudal system eventually arose.

Ironically, by destroying Ostrogothic rule the Byzantines opened Italy up to eventual conquest by invaders far more barbaric—the Teutonic tribesmen known as the Lombards. Their aim was to annex the whole peninsula, but the Lombards never did succeed in gaining possession of either the Duchy of Rome, held by the pope, or Naples and the stretch of coast at the boot of Italy, though they did have the satisfaction of finally wresting Ravenna from the Byzantines. Their ruthless policy was to dispossess the existing landlords and make their serfs and slaves work for them instead. The invaders were the only freemen; the rest, whatever their previous rank, were bondsmen. In approximately 570 Florence fell to the Lombards and their leader Alboin. In due course he was to conquer the whole of Tuscany.

As inevitably happens in such cases, the invaders not only changed their country of adoption but also

were changed by it. They first learned the strange language and then gave up their own for it. Near the close of the seventh century, the royal family abandoned the Arianism they had held in common with the Ostrogoths and made their submission to the pope, accepting the consubstantiality of Christ. Also inevitably, their subjects followed their example, and in this way the dominant minority was gradually fused with the majority it dominated. As the Lombards had first come to adopt the alien language and the alien form of Christianity, so they later came to adopt alien customs and modes of dress, even reviving the moribund judicial system. Out of this fusion between invaders and original inhabitants can be said to have sprung the northern Italy of today. Remarkably enough, the demarcation between northern Italy and the papal domains and southern Italy, first established by the Lombard conquests, has survived into the present, with many bitter consequences for a country still seeking to be truly united.

A succession of Lombard dukes used Florence both as a military camp and as a trading center, but their city must have been a squalid place in comparison both with the Roman city before it and the Renaissance city that was to follow. Nonetheless, the Lombards did found several churches during this period, among them the Baptistery and Or San Michele, the original building of which was replaced in the fourteenth century by the structure we see today. In addition, they erected one of their characteristic watchtowers on the site where the Palazzo Vecchio was later to be built, to guard the approaches from the east.

Two centuries of Lombard rule came to an end when Charlemagne—that "Carlo Magno" whose soul, in Dante's *Paradiso*, finds an honored place in the heaven of Mars—crossed the Alps to assist his papal ally, Adrian, who was finding himself under increasing pressure from the new Lombard king, Desiderius. In 774 Charlemagne defeated Desiderius and seized his kingdom for himself.

The Lombards had ruled through *duces*, or dukes—and also, in later years, through officials called *gestaldi*, over whom the king could exert more stringent control. Charlemagne replaced both with his *comities*, or counts (*conti*, in Italian), ascribing to each a *contado*, or fief. Because Florence had sunk into such insignificance during the centuries after the fall of the Roman empire, a chronicler like Villani and a poet like Dante were tempted to exaggerate Charlemagne's role as the Fairy Prince, arousing the Sleeping Beauty of their native city from her long slumber. It was claimed not merely that he spent considerable time within her boundaries, during which he extended her *contado* to a radius of three miles around the Baptistery, but also that he gave such an impulse to the rebuilding and readornment of the city that he can almost be regarded as its second founder. The Romanesque church of SS. Apostoli, though its present structure clearly dates from the eleventh century, is said to have been built by him—a fact commemorated on its façade—and similiar claims, also disputed, have been made for S. Stefano al Ponte and S. Trinita.

The usual reason given for the dissolution of the Frankish empire is that none of Charlemagne's suc-

The interior of the Baptistery is undeniably striking, with its inlays of black and white marble surmounted by a glittering mosaic depicting scenes from the Old and New Testaments, but it is the exterior of this octagonal fourteenth-century structure that has made it world-famous. Specifically, it is the bronze doors on the south, north, and east sides of the Baptistery that draw tens of thousands of art lovers to Florence every year. In any other setting the south door, the work of Andrea Pisano (detail at left, below) would be held an unparalleled achievement. Here, unhappily, they must compete against the north door, created by Lorenzo Ghiberti in the twenty years after he was declared the winner of a now-legendary competition that also involved Donatello and Brunelleschi, among others—and both are overshadowed by the stupendous east door, a twenty-seven-year labor of love on Ghiberti's part that Michelangelo declared, on seeing it completed, was worthy to serve as the gateway to Paradise.

cessors had his charm, authority, and genius. But a reason no less important was the revival of commerce after centuries of torpor. As a consequence, cities such as Florence, suddenly resuscitated, had a new sense of belonging, not to a vast and nebulous empire in a state of deliquescence, but to a small area in a state of furious growth. After that long, lethargic interregnum when, if existence changed at all, it changed for the worse, there was an upsurge of hope and energy. Previously abandoned land was reclaimed for cultivation; men assiduously dug canals to drain the marshes, facilitate transport, and provide irrigation; and the movement of dismayed city-dwellers from the towns into the country was sharply reversed. As a result of all this, the population of Florence rapidly increased.

Extremely important to the later emergence of the Tuscan city states was the appointment, under the last of the Carolignian emperors, of an official with the title of margrave. From his initial residence in Lucca, this lord, who was almost a sovereign, ruled the rest of Tuscany through deputies who bore the title of vice-count. When the emperor was strong, the margrave would go through the pretense of deferring to his authority; when he was weak, as he increasingly tended to be, the margrave ignored him. Similarly, a strong margrave would keep his vice-counts strictly subservient to him, while a weak one would allow them to behave as semi-independent heads of government.

In this period—the tenth and eleventh centuries—when the central administration was often little more than fiction, the authority that mattered most

was local authority. That local authority might be lodged not merely with the vice-count of the district but with some powerful cleric or army officer. These separate elements were constantly at loggerheads, and in the confusion that resulted, feudalism—described by the historian Ferdinand Schevill as "a system of order in disorder"—became entrenched. The vassal, unprotected by the emperor, entered into a compact with his local lord; the two became inextricably bound to each other in mutual support.

In the haphazard, ill-organized surge of commercial activity that swept through Italy in the late Middle Ages, Florence found itself in a particularly strong position. Her location astride the Flaminian Road, the great highway that crossed northern Italy, was highly favorable to her trade. Moreover, German emperors on their way south to be crowned by the current Vicar of Christ would lodge in her palaces. And in their turn this or that pope would find Florence a convenient and comfortable place of refuge when the Eternal City became too turbulent.

This increasing prosperity led to the construction of a number of buildings. Reference has already been made to the Baptistery, known in Italian as the Battisterio di San Giovanni, the oldest of them all. This octagonal edifice was probably erected by the Lombards in the sixth or seventh century, although there is a tradition that it dates back to Roman times. It was then remodeled in Romanesque style near the end of the eleventh century, largely at the expense of the wealthy Arte di Calimala, or Guild of Foreign Cloth. An apse was added where the altar stands now, and the center of the cupola, which had

previously been open to the sky like that of the Pantheon in Rome, was closed in with a lantern. After 1108, each child born in Florence was brought to the Baptistery to be made a Christian. A rough-and-ready register of the numbers and the sex of these children was kept during the late Middle Ages by dropping beans into a vase—a white bean for a girl and a black bean for a boy.

Another building of this same period is the church of San Miniato al Monte, founded by Bishop Aldibrando (Hildebrand), a pioneer of medieval architecture, in 1013 and dedicated to the Greek martyr Minias. The bones of this saint now rest in the crypt of the church, having been moved there from a little tabernacle erected in honor of St. Peter in the nearby Val di Botte, which was known in Minias's day as Arisbotta. The legend is that Minias lived as a hermit in Arisbotta until he was seized, dragged across the Arno into Florence, and there decapitated. Miraculously, his headless body then rose up, recrossed the Arno by the only bridge then in existence, and laid itself out among the martyrs already buried in the tabernacle of St. Peter.

Standing outside the walls of Florence, high above the Arno, San Miniato is the beautiful church about which Dante wrote in a famous passage in *The Divine Comedy*:

> . . . *La chiesa che soggioga*
> *La ben guidata sopra Rubaconte*
> . . . *The church that dominates*
> *The auspicious crossing by the Rubaconte bridge*

It was his parish church.

The exterior, with its marble inlays, dates from two centuries after the building was erected, and is generally thought to be inferior to the rest. The campanile, the successor to one that collapsed in 1499, may owe its survival to Michelangelo, who, when Florence was under siege in 1529, supervised its lagging with mattresses as a precaution against damage from cannonballs.

Within, by an arrangement unusual in Tuscany, the nave leads directly to the crypt, with the sanctuary above it. This necessitates approaching the latter by flights of steps from the side aisles. Ironically, the walls are faced, in many cases, with marble slabs removed from temples of those heathen gods whom Minias had been martyred for refusing to worship. The little Chapel of the Crucifix—commissioned by Piero dei Medici in 1448 and designed by Michelozzo—which stands at the end of the nave, has associated with it a touching story regarding Giovanni Gualberti, the eleventh-century founder of the Vallombrosan order of monks. (Gualberti's painted cross, now removed to S. Trinita, once rested in the chapel.) One Good Friday, Gualberti, then still a layman, was walking with some friends on the hill immediately below the church when he met the murderer of his brother Hugo. Gualberti at once drew a dagger, but the murderer, who was alone, pleaded for mercy, reminding him that this was the day Christ had died on the cross. To the amazement of his companions, the future saint put away his dagger and entered the church, where he knelt before the Crucifix. As he remained there in prayer, Christ suddenly looked down at him and nodded in com-

mendation. Gualberti resolved, after this mystical experience, to forsake the world and become a monk—and so founded the Vallombrosan order.

The historical facts, as we know them, are less romantic but more credible. Of noble birth, Gualberti had first become a soldier. Then, after being drawn into the seething religious conflicts of his day, he decided that his vocation lay in the church and entered the new monastery of San Miniato. There he found that his abbot, Hubert, was a corrupt priest who owed his appointment by the equally corrupt Bishop of Florence, Hatto, not to sanctity but to bribery and favoritism. An impulsive man of considerable courage, Gualberti at once began to denounce his superior, not merely within the order but publicly. Soon his street-corner denunciations encompassed other priests whom he regarded as equally unworthy of their calling. After he had been the cause of a brawl in the Mercato Vecchio—during which he was badly beaten up—Gualberti took himself off to Vallombrosa, today a summer resort amid pinewoods popular with the Florentines, and there melded a heterogeneous collection of young and enthusiastic supporters into an order of his own. This order soon spread throughout the whole of Tuscany, enabling Gualberti to continue to prosecute his campaign against ecclesiastical corruption, simony, and concubinage with the utmost vigor. By the time of his death in 1073, he had found a powerful ally in the newly elected pope, Gregory VII, who was eventually to come into conflict with the emperor on precisely the subject of the demarcation between temporal and spiritual powers.

Before his succession to the papacy, Gregory VII, whose name was then Hildebrand, had put forward the revolutionary proposal that the pope should be appointed not by the emperor, as he had been in the past, but by a College of Cardinals. A decree to this effect was promulgated in 1059 by Pope Nicholas II, and it is still in force today. In 1075 Hildebrand, by now Pope Gregory VII, promulgated another decree, this one forbidding any temporal ruler, under pain of excommunication, to invest a cleric. Needless to say, the youthful emperor, Henry IV, vigorously opposed this abolition of lay investiture. He announced that he was deposing Gregory—and Gregory retaliated by excommunicating the emperor.

In this conflict, which divided the whole of Italy, Florence took sides with the pope. The chief reason for this alignment was the Florentines' devotion to Countess Matilda, margrave of Tuscany. Only one Tuscan margrave before her had earned as much love and respect from the Florentines. In her progresses about her domains, she showed a clear preference for her residence behind the Bargello in Florence, and in consequence *Le Laude di Matelda*—"Matilda's Songs of Praise"—were chanted in the Florentine churches, and parents named their daughters Contessa or Tessa in her honor. Dante, who did not share her political views, nonetheless represented her in *The Divine Comedy* as the Lady of Earthly Paradise, the active life of the soul, in contrast to Beatrice, who represented the passive life.

The reasons why Matilda herself decided to take the part of the pope, when she might more naturally have sided with her overlord, the emperor, are also interesting. In the Florentine hagiography of the period immediately succeeding her death, Matilda was represented as a serene, withdrawn, saintlike figure whose devotion to a life of religious contemplation made her sympathetic to the papal cause. On the other hand, English biographers of the nineteenth century tended to see her as a kind of medieval Queen Victoria, at once firm, devout, gracious, cultivated, and ladylike. In fact, she was a far more complex and fascinating character than either of these two images may suggest.

As an extremely young girl Matilda had been obliged to marry her stepfather's hunchback son, one Godfrey, Duke of Upper Lotharingia, and take up residence with him beyond the Alps, far from the mother, Beatrice, to whom she was deeply attached. After the death of her only child soon after birth, she returned to Tuscany. Thenceforward she and her husband, whom she clearly found repulsive, lived apart—and after his assassination in 1076 she did not seek another mate. Her stepfather having died, Matilda had ruled Tuscany with her mother from 1069 until 1076, after which she ruled alone. *Le gran Contessa*, as her contemporaries called her, was neither a religious recluse nor a woman of delicate femininity. She led her troops, armor-clad; she took as much pleasure in hunting as any man; and even the most powerful of her lords were expected to kneel when addressing her. Yet without any doubt she was genuinely pious, and one can infer that this piety was a substitute for the love of husband and children that, whether by choice or by circumstance, she had failed to achieve.

If we count the period of her co-reign with her mother, Matilda ruled Tuscany for almost half a century. During this period the steadily increasing prosperity of the towns of northern Italy brought more and more power to a new urban class whose chief characteristics were acquisitiveness, devoutness, and civic pride. As proof of the growing independence of Florence, we have the record of an unnamed annalist that in 1107 the Florentines destroyed the neighboring castle of Monte Cascioli. Such military operations represented attempts to prevent the surrounding feudal lords from continuing to interfere in the commercial life of the ever-expanding city. They also demonstrate that by this time, near the close of her reign, the authority of Matilda, by now aging and enfeebled, had declined. After her death Florence was to undertake military expeditions not only against outnumbered enemies but also against rival cities. Prato was subjected in 1107; Fiesole, in 1125; and Figline and Empoli soon met with a similar fate.

It was during the latter half of the eleventh century and throughout the twelfth that communal rule really began to supersede that of the margrave and his *conti*. This communal rule evolved slowly but inexorably. At first the members of a parish would meet after Sunday mass to discuss problems of common interest: the maintenance of the roads, repairs to the church, the care of the sick, aged, and destitute. There followed the inevitable development that, when a number of parishes had some problem in common, they decided to cooperate. Each then selected a representative, empowered to speak on behalf of his parish. These representatives were known first as *boni homines*—the Latin equivalent of the "good men and true" of the Anglo-Saxon jury—and then, more grandiloquently, as consuls, after the Roman pattern. Their term of office usually lasted for a year and, in general, they came from one of three classes of citizens: knights, or *milites*, who had always been residents of Florence, even if they owned estates outside it; nobles, who had moved into Florence after being subjected by the Florentines; and rich merchants, who had usually married into one or another of the two classes above them.

Some writers have presented these communes as models of selfless cooperation, but as in civic government in most countries of the world today, there were cabals, feuds, rivalries, conspiracies, and corruption as well as genuine solidarity and altruism. Families tended to band together, one against the rest; and as material manifestations of this aggressiveness, stone towers, many more than a hundred feet high, rose all over the city. By the end of the twelfth century more than two hundred such towers were in existence, but few are now still standing, and those that are appear considerably reduced in height as a result of a thirteenth-century civic enactment. When the nobles formed an association to resist the upward thrust of the populace, it was named *La Societa delle Torre*—"The Tower Society," and the phrase "families of towers and loggias"—came to be used in the sense of "the upper crust."

The ideal place in Florence to view the remaining examples of these towers is from a window in the Sala del Niobe in the Uffizi Gallery: those of the

In the thirty-first canto of the **Inferno** Dante relates that when he reached the lowest circle of Hell on his imaginary tour of the underworld the light was so dim that he was barely able to distinguish form from shadow. In the gloom he momentarily mistook the giants standing around Lucifer for **alte torri**—"high towers" —and there can be little question that he had in mind the skyscape of his native city as seen in the last light of day. Since Dante's time most of these high towers, symbols of familial pride and commercial aggressiveness, have been pulled down, but a few—like the one below —do survive, reminders of a time when hundreds of these stone towers cast their long shadows over the city.

OVERLEAF: The skyscape of modern Florence is dominated by, from left to right in this panoramic view: the dome of Santa Maria Novella, completed in 1360; Giotto's airy, elegant campanile for the Cathedral of Santa Maria del Fiore, known universally as the Duomo; Brunelleschi's massive dome for that same structure; the needle-like spire of the Palazzo Vecchio, rising 300 feet above the Piazza della Signoria; and, beyond a smaller, Gothic spire, the squat, crenelated tower of the Bargello.

Gherardini, Acciaiuloli, and Baldovinetti families are visible in a single glance. Other towers can be found in Via Lambertasca, the Borgo Santissimi Apostoli, and the Borgo San Jacopo. But it is, of course, in the neighboring town of San Gemignano that one can best appreciate, in what resembles a giant bamboo grove of towers, what Florence must once have looked like. From these towers, and later from the palazzi, with their machicolated battlements and narrow windows, a cry of *Accor' uomo!*— "Help, help!"—would bring men swooping down into the street to join the fray.

From time to time, the progress of Florence toward complete self-determination would receive a sudden check. The emperor would cross the Alps from his German to his Italian domains, where his liege lords would complain to him about these impertinent encroachments on their authority. The reigns of Frederick Barbarossa and of his tough and able son, Henry VI, were particularly repressive for the cities of Tuscany—which, unlike those of Lombardy, had formed no association for their mutual protection. But on the death of Henry VI in 1197, they finally took the first steps in forming such an association, and the beginning of the new century was thus one of hope for them. The new emperor was a child of only three, and feuding in Germany was so intense that there was grave doubt whether, on reaching manhood, he would ascend the throne.

It must have seemed to the Commune of Florence, then, that the feudal authority of the emperor had been broken decisively and irreparably. But the struggle for independence was by no means over.

43

III

Enemies Without, Enemies Within

It was not until 1208, when Philip of Swabia, the brother of Henry VI, was assassinated, that one man again assumed sole control of the empire. That man was Otto of Saxony—who was elected by his peers, and subsequently crowned by the pope, on the solemn vow that he would make no claim to the southern Kingdom of Sicily, of which Henry VI had gained possession through a dynastic marriage. Immediately after his coronation, however, Otto IV, as he was now known, hastened to reassert imperial authority in Tuscany and then, with an extraordinary combination of bad faith and miscalculation, set out to conquer Sicily. The pope immediately summoned Henry VI's son Frederick, by then eighteen, from Germany to Rome, and urged him to wrest the crown from Otto. This Frederick eventually succeeded in doing, but the papal task took three years—and with the two contenders absent across the Alps and wholly absorbed in their conflict, the towns of Tuscany, with Florence in the forefront, found themselves in the happy position of being able, once again, to control their separate destinies.

From the rivalry between Frederick II and Otto IV sprang the murderous feud between Guelphs and Ghibellines that was repeatedly to divide Italy in general and Florence in particular for decades to come. The word Guelph derived from Welf, the family name of Otto IV; the word Ghibelline, from a castle belonging to Frederick's family, the Hohenstaufen, in Waiblingen. When Frederick's troops charged they would shout "Waiblingen!"—and this was transmuted by the Italians, clearly no better linguists then than now, into "Ghibellino."

At first, while Frederick II was still the pope's youthful protégé, it was the Ghibellines who were regarded as the papal party; but this brilliant and resourceful character, thought to have had more sympathy with Islam than with Christianity and eventually known as *Stupor Mundi*—"The Wonder of the World," had soon made an enemy of his former ally through his determination to reimpose imperial hegemony in northern Italy. As a result, it was the Guelphs who eventually became the party of the pope, and the Ghibellines that of the emperor. It must not be inferred from this that the pope had any sympathy with the system of communal self-government that had gradually emerged in Tuscany during the previous century; but he cannily preferred to be surrounded by a number of city-states, rather than be straddled by an imperial power entrenched both south of him in Sicily and north of him in Lombardy and Tuscany.

The conflicts between emperor and pope and between the old feudal system and the new system of communal independence did not end until the death of Frederick II in 1250. By then Florence was dramatically divided in its allegiances. The cause of this rift, as Dante and his contemporaries relate it, dates from 1215, when Buondelmonte dei Buondelmonti, scion of a noble family driven into Florence after the destruction of their castle of Montebuoni in Val di Greve, was betrothed to the daughter of another noble family, the Amidei, in order to heal a long-standing feud. At the last moment the impulsive youth broke his troth and announced that, instead, he would marry a beautiful young girl named

Ciulla Donati. This, with an extreme lack of tact, he proposed to do on the very day when he should have married the Amidei girl.

As the young bridegroom, dressed in white and on a white palfrey, was riding across the Ponte Vecchio for the ceremony at his family's palazzo in Borgo Santissimi Apostoli, the Amadei, with their *consorzeria*, or allies, among the powerful Uberti clan, set upon him. They first clubbed and then stabbed him to death, leaving his corpse, with grim symbolism, beneath the statue of Mars at the foot of the bridge. Later his corpse was carried through Florence, with the bereaved Donati girl supporting the head of her betrothed on his sumptuous bier. What appeared to be no more than an act of private vengeance for a slight to one family's honor soon embroiled the whole city, some noble families siding with the Buondelmonti and others banding together under the Uberti. The first faction declared themselves Guelphs, the second Ghibellines.

Such, at any rate, is the traditional story. But as so often is the case when a deep division suddenly appears in the fabric of society, it would be wrong to mistake the occasion for the cause. There was already bitter dissension among the leading families of the city, long before headstrong youth met adorable maiden, and the affair of the jilted girl and the murdered boy only served to bring that dissension into focus and polarize it. Each faction wished to control the city. The Ghibellines, under the leadership of the oldest and proudest of the noble families, looked to the emperor to establish and maintain them in sole power; the Guelphs, many of

them drawn from families that had more recently come to the fore, looked to the pope to fulfill the same role. What they were to continue to quarrel about for almost two centuries was not an act of bad faith but something far more important: sovereignty. Between 1237 and 1250, power seesawed between the two sides as the fortunes of emperor and pope seesawed. Guelphs would drive Ghibellines out of the city and seize or destroy their property; Ghibellines would return in due course and do precisely the same to Guelphs.

While the nobles quarreled with such savagery, a powerful bourgeoisie, eager to protect itself and its commerical interests, formed an anti-aristocratic grouping called the *popolo*. In response to the feuds among the nobles, a new office of *podestà* had already been created. The *podestà*, whose title derived from the Latin *potestas*, meaning power, served as a single executive in place of the numerous consuls of the twelfth century. His term of office lasted one year and, in order to ensure that he was entirely impartial in adjudicating between opposing factions, he was not a Florentine but a man from some other city. With the death of Frederick II in 1250, the seesaw of power tipped again—and the Guelphs slid back into power, inaugurating a decade of relative political stability known as *Il Primo Popolo*, the First Democracy. When it came into being the Florentines built for the *podestà* a residence known first as the Palazzo del Podestà but later as the Bargello (because, during the reign of Cosimo I, it became both the house of the *bargello*, or chief of police, and also the prison of the city).

This grim building, composed of massive free-stone blocks quarried at Fiesole and Gonfolina on the Arno, stands in Via del Proconsulo, a street so narrow that it is difficult to view the structure's façade properly. In any case, its real beauty is revealed only after one enters the gate and sees the *cortile,* or inner courtyard, and the elegantly proportioned outside staircase.

During the decade of *Il Primo Popolo,* Florence was ruled by the *podestà* in conjunction with an official, also from another city, called the Capitano del Popolo, who acted as military leader of the twenty companies into which the citizenry formed themselves for war. A lot of power at this period also rested with the *Anziani* (ancients), a representative body of twelve men, two for each of the wards into which the city was divided.

Though now a democratic republic, the city had in no way relinquished the expansionist ambitions fostered by its rapidly growing economy and population. All Tuscany, it was declared, must be Guelph and under the control of Florence. Inevitably, the Ghibellines, whose chief strongholds were Siena and Pisa, resisted this aim—although with scant success. At the conclusion of the Guelph campaign in 1254—called forever afterward "the year of victory" by the Florentines—Florence had indeed established virtual hegemony over Tuscany.

In their battles against the forces of Pistoia, Siena, and Pisa, the Florentines would muster under twenty standards, each led by a *gonfalonier,* or standard-bearer, who, like the *podestà* and the Capitano del Popolo, was elected for a single year. The Caroccio,

a huge platform on four wheels that supported the standard of Florence and a bell, would accompany them, drawn by one or more pairs of oxen decorated with scarlet trappings. This vehicle, cumbersome as a London double-decker bus, would be the Florentines' rallying point, its bell never silent until victory was theirs.

The Caroccio, along with the supremacy it symbolized, was lost by Florence on September 12, 1260, under the walls of Siena in the battle of Montaperti. There were two reasons for this defeat. The first and more important was that Manfred, illegitimate son of the late Frederick II, had seized the throne of Sicily in 1258. Elated by this event, the Ghibellines had staged a revolt in Florence and then, when it proved unsuccessful, had precipitately fled the city. In alliance with the Sienese, these Ghibellines-in-exile sent emissaries to Manfred, asking for his help. Manfred responded by dispatching a body of German troops under the command of a relative of his, Count Giordano. A brilliant cavalry charge by this army tipped the scales in their favor, despite the Florentines' numerical superiority.

The second cause of the Florentine defeat was the treachery of certain of the Florentine forces, secretly Ghibelline in their sympathies, who, as soon as the battle started, either took to their heels or set on their fellow citizens—instead of on the Sienese and Germans. Chief among the traitors was Mocca degli Abbati, whom Dante describes as tearing the hair from his scalp, in the pit of traitors in Hell, such is his guilt at having lopped off the hand of a Florentine standard-bearer.

As soon as news reached Florence of the catastrophe at Siena, a catastrophe in which almost every family had lost at least one member, there was such panic and consternation that, instead of manning the defenses of the city, the leading Guelph families fled to exile in Lucca. At a conference in Empoli, the Ghibellines debated whether or not to destroy Florence; that the city was spared was due only to the eloquent pleading of Farinata degli Uberti, who had played a heroic role in the battle—on the Sienese side. "The city," he declared, "ungrateful as it has been to my house, is dear to my heart, and my sword shall defend it to the death." Count Giordano was so moved by these words that he seconded the veto. Ironically, the savior of Florence was subsequently killed by a Buondelmonte in an engagement between Ghibellines and Guelphs near Lucca.

The Ghibellines were to hold Florence until 1267. The cause of their ousting was the defeat and death in battle, at Beneventum, of their champion, Manfred, who had been successfully challenged for the throne of Sicily by the younger brother of Louis IX of France, Charles of Anjou. One French pope, Urban IV, had been succeeded in 1265 by another, Clement IV, and it was natural that, in their anti-Hohenstaufen policy, both should favor a compatriot. After Manfred's death, one might have expected to see the Ghibellines immediately expelled from Florence. This is certainly what Pope Clement expected; but the *popolani*, who had resumed political control of the city, felt secure enough to take the attitude of "A plague on both your houses"—and made no attempt to drive out the vanquished Ghibellines.

Clement therefore decided that force would be needed and, making Charles of Anjou his vice-regent in Tuscany, sent him to subdue the intransigent city. Surprisingly, the Ghibellines offered scant resistance. And so it came to pass that French arms assisted one faction, the Guelphs, to replace another faction, the Ghibellines, whom German arms had assisted to power. It was, by coincidence, on the fifty-first anniversary of the murder of Buondelmonte, an Easter Sunday, that Florence again passed to the Guelphs. But the new government was far less democratic than *Il Primo Popolo* of a decade previously, being composed of nobles and those leading merchant families that had formed alliances with them through marriage.

An economic boom followed the restoration of peace to the city. The chief item of trade at this period, finished fabric, depended on skillful redressing, by a special process, of coarse woollen cloth imported from France and England. The powerful Arte della Lana, or Guild of Wool, built for itself a magnificent hall, still to be seen in Via di Calimala, close to Or San Michele. It had for its coat of arms a lamb with a flag and a wool-comb—and the Florentine *giglio*, or lily, above in a red field. Scarcely less powerful was the Arte di Calimala, or Guild of Foreign Cloth, which for two hundred years ran the city's first postal service in addition to being responsible for the upkeep of many churches and hospitals.

Even where the guild halls have vanished, street names still recall them. It was in the present Via Calzaioli (Stocking-makers Street) that the Guild of Hosiers had many factories and shops; the Guild of

Furriers and Skinners had quarters in the present Via Pelicceria (Leather-makers Street). A visitor to Borgo degli Albizzi may still see, on some of the window frames of Palazzo Alessandri, the rods on which the cloth of the Arte di Calimala was hung out to dry. If nineteenth-century England was a nation of shopkeepers, then medieval Florence was a republic of merchants.

Commerce at this period was greatly assisted by the stability of the *fiorino d'oro*, or gold florin, first struck in the mint that used to stand on the site of the present Uffizi. Previously, Florentine coins had been made only of bronze or silver. The *fiorino d'oro* bore on one side the image of John the Baptist, patron of the city, and on the other the *giglio*. It contained twenty-four carats of unalloyed gold and was not only accepted throughout Italy but became the model of gold coinage in France, Spain, and England. (Indeed, the word "florin" was in use in England until the introduction of decimal coinage.) So great became the demand for the *fiorino* that by the close of the thirteenth century the mint was turning out no less than 400,000 annually; and so scrupulously did the Florentines safeguard its purity that Dante placed in Hell the spirit of Maestro Adamo, who had adulterated coins while serving at the mint.

In a city so dependent on commerce, it was inevitable that the guilds would come to exercise greater and greater power. As a result of the intervention of Pope Nicholas, who had dispatched his nephew, Cardinal Datino, to Tuscany in order to bring about a reconciliation between the two opposing factions, Ghibellines had been permitted to return to Flor-

51

ence in 1280, when they were given back their former properties, many now no more than heaps of rubble. Datino presented Florence with a new constitution, in which the two sides were to cooperate in the city government; but the Guelphs, who were now in a totally dominant position over the disheartened and often impoverished Ghibellines, swept it away after two years and promulgated a constitution of their own. It was based on the guilds, on whom the prosperity of the city so largely depended.

In Florence in 1280 there were, in addition to the seven Greater Guilds (*Arti maggiori*), at least twenty-five Lesser Guilds (*Arti miniori*). The Judges and Notaries came first in the list of Greater Guilds, followed by the Dressers of Foreign Cloth, the Money Changers, the Wool Manufacturers, the Silk Merchants, the Doctors and Apothecaries, and the Skinners and Furriers. Each of these Greater Guilds had its own band of soldiers, presided over by a *gonfalonier*, so that collectively they formed an army, always ready to leap to the defense of the Republic. The Lesser Guilds took in such members of the petite bourgeoisie as the Butchers, Shoemakers, Builders, and Armorers.

It was the Greater Guilds that, in effect, took over the government of the city in 1382, since it was from their numbers that the six priors were chosen who ruled together for a brief but intense two-month period of office. While engaged on this duty, they lived communally, first in a mansion hired for this purpose and then, after it had been built, in the Palazzo Vecchio. The *podestà*, still a foreigner, remained, to act as chief magistrate and commander of the army;

but he was now subordinate to the priors—or Signoria, as they came collectively to be designated.

The wisest of *podestàs* seems to have been a man called Rubaconte, who, having come from Como in 1236 to assume the office, soon earned the reputation of a Solomon. On one occasion, a simple-minded bathhouse proprietor, Bagnai, was dragged before him by the angry members of a family who declared that he had killed one of their own. It appeared that Bagnai had been crossing the extremely narrow bridge over the Arno when a party of horsemen had come prancing toward him. To avoid being crushed to death, he had clambered onto the wooden railing; but even there he had not been safe, since one of the horses had brushed against him, toppling him into the river. By ill chance, he had fallen onto the head of a man who was washing his feet in the water below, and it was this unfortunate, not he, who had died.

After some deliberation, Rubaconte agreed that the family honor must be vindicated and the injury avenged. The accused must go and wash his feet on precisely the same spot, and a member of the aggrieved family was accorded the privilege of falling over the railing of the bridge on top of him. Needless to say, not one of them was willing to volunteer for this honor.

Afterwards, Rubaconte began to think of the dangers of a bridge so narrow, and he eventually persuaded the priors that a wider one must be built. At a cermonial inauguration, he himself carried the first basket of mortar; and the bridge, completed in 1236, was named the Ponte Rubaconte.

Like Venice, Florence was a center of culture because it was a city of commerce, not because it was the capital of an empire. It was the merchant guilds that provided what little civil continuity Florence could boast of during the protracted internecine squabbling between the Guelph and Ghibelline factions; and it was the so-called Arti maggiori, *or Greater Guilds, that became the de facto government of Florence in 1382, providing the city with the first real domestic stability it had known in centuries. Of these Greater Guilds, none was as vital to Florentine commercial interests as the* Arte della Lana, *the Wool Manufacturers' Guild. It created the fine cloth that Florence exported to all of Europe—and that income, in turn, provided commissions to the city's many artists. Commerce and culture combine in the guild's medallion, which is attributed to Luca della Robbia.*

It was this same Rubaconte who caused to be laid down the handsome polygonal flagstones that survive today in the center of the city. One of his sayings, expressing a humanity unusual at that period—"Law must be tempered with discretion"—has achieved proverbial status in Italy. At the end of his term of office, his honesty, impartiality, and keen judgment were amply rewarded. Not only did he return to Como laden with gifts and honors, but his shield was painted on the house that he had occupied in the Via Bardi, near the bridge that had been erected through his efforts.

The thirteenth century was a great one for the founding of charitable confraternities; but the motive was not, as it usually is today, a philanthropic desire to save others' lives so much as the prudent one of saving one's own soul. Some of these confraternities have survived into the present. The Misericordia, which, after the passage of so many centuries, can still be seen transporting and caring for the sick and attending to the disposal of the dead, is said to have come into being when Piero Borsi, a humble porter employed by the Arte di Calimala, suggested to his fellow workers that each time one of them swore, the blasphemer should make a donation for the sick. Today there are more than 450 chapters of the Misericordia in every part of Tuscany. Its members still give at least one hour of their time each week for nothing, and all its funds still come from private sources. But today they maintain their anonymity with hoods, cloaks, and masks of black rather than the traditional scarlet.

The Compagnia di S. Maria del Bigallo is almost as old. Their headquarters, opposite the cathedral belltower, contains a chapel with an altar by Andrea della Robbia and a statue of the patron saint of the confraternity, Sebastian, by Benedetto da Maiano. The Bigallo was built on the site of the Guarda Morto—a tall tower so named because it overlooked what was then a burial ground around the Baptistery and may even, some think, have been used for the accommodation of bodies before their interment. In 1248, when the Ghibellines were in control of the city, they decided that the Guarda Morto, which belonged to a Guelph family, should be pulled down together with a number of other towers owned by Guelphs. And because the Baptistery was a Guelph meeting place, Ghibellines planned to have the tower collapse on top of it—despite the fact that the Baptistery was then revered as a monument from Roman times. However, a miracle occurred. As the fourteenth-century chronicler Villani put it: "As it pleased God and St. John, the tower fell in the middle of the piazza, and it was manifest that the tower was turned full round to avoid falling as ordained." Skeptics are more likely to ascribe the survival of the baptistery to the skill of Niccola Pisano, who was in charge of the demolition and who, as an artist, would have respected a building of such elegance.

Whereas the Misericordia expanded over the centuries, becoming the Italian equivalent of the Red Cross, the Bigallo has shrunk. Its chief function immediately after World War II was to remove from the streets and find homes for the numbers of children who wandered around begging insistently, usually from foreigners. Now such child beggars are

The great Franciscan church of Santa Croce is the Westminster Abbey
of Florence, as famous for its tombs as its frescoes. In Childe
Harold's Pilgrimage Byron takes note of the illustrious entombed:

> In Santa Croce's holy precincts lie
> Ashes which make it holier, dust which is
> Even in itself an immortality,
> Though there was nothing save the past, and this,
> The particle of those sublimities
> Which have relapsed to chaos; here repose
> Angelo's, Alfieri's bones, and his,
> The starry Galileo, with his woes;
> Here Machiavelli's earth, return'd to whence it rose.

Unhappily, these many tombs—Michelangelo's and Ghiberti's among
them—obscure the frescoes with which Giotto covered the interior.
Portions are still visible, however, as are the della Robbia medallions,
such as the one at right, that grace the Pazzi Chapel of Santa Croce.

55

few, and the attention of the order is concentrated on the indigent aged, of whom there are many.

Another confraternity that came into existence at about this time was the first foundling hospital, built in 1218 at the expense of Giudalotto de Volto dall' Orco, an eminent citizen of the day. Originally it stood outside the walls of the city, near the Porta San Gallo, and was dedicated to Our Lady. In 1294, the Guild of Silk Merchants took the confraternity under its patronage, and nearly two hundred years later this early hospital was incorporated with the new Ospedale degli Innocenti, erected between 1419 and 1426 by Brunelleschi in the Piazza dei Servi. The most casual passerby cannot fail to be attracted by the exterior of this building, its loggia decorated with exquisite medallions of swaddled infants by Andrea della Robbia.

In the foundation of these charitable institutions the influence of the great religious orders of the Dominicans and the Franciscans must be acknowledged, even if, by the close of the thirteenth century, the ideals of the founders tended to be forgotten by their spiritual descendants. No two characters could be more different than the ardent and energetic Spaniard, Dominic, who was dedicated to holding Christians, by force and even torture if need be, to the strictest orthodoxy, and the gentle native of Assisi, Francis, who regarded belief as a consequence of a personal search for God, who preached love toward all creatures, and who abjured all worldly pomp and power. To Dante, Dominic was *l'amoroso drudo della fede cristiana*—"the passionate lover of the faith of Christ." To preserve that faith, his fol-

lowers conducted the Inquisition. In an exquisite passage elsewhere in *The Divine Comedy,* Dante describes the mystical marriage of St. Francis with his bride, Poverty.

The chief Dominican church of Florence is Santa Maria Novella, which stands a little to the southwest of the Baptistery. The building was begun in 1278, on a site that, before the erection of a third circle of walls around Florence, was actually outside the city boundaries. As a result, the church was first known as Santa Maria tra le Vigne, or St. Mary among the Vineyards. Since the Dominican friars were the great preachers of that period, attracting the kinds of crowds that nowadays flock to hear a Billy Graham, the nave is wide and unencumbered with monuments. This is one of the most beautiful of the Florentine churches, with frescoes by Andrea and Bernardo Orcagna in the Strozzi Chapel, a wooden crucifix by Brunelleschi in the Gondi Chapel, and, in the Rucellai Chapel, Giovanni Cimabue's *Madonna,* of which Elizabeth Barrett Browning wrote:

A noble picture! worthy of the shout
Wherewith along the streets the people bore
Its cherub-faces, which the sun threw out,
Until they stopped and entered the church door.

The first settlement of the Franciscans dates from the year 1211. It was then that Francis, his rule still unconfirmed by the pope, visited Florence, staying with a little band of his followers in a house outside the Porta San Gallo. After seventy years or so, the Altafronti family gave the order the site on which Santa Croce now stands, and Franciscans migrated

there to build a chapel and monastery dedicated to St. Antony. Some parts of this original edifice remain behind the choir of the later church, which was begun, to designs of Arnolfo del Cambio, in the year 1294. Two of the great guilds, the Arte dei Mercanti and the Arte di Calimala, contributed to the building funds and, after Cardinal Matteo d'Acquasparta proclaimed an indulgence for any private individual who also provided financial support, many of the richest families of the city—the Alberti, Baroncelli, Bardi, Cerchi, Peruzzi—also became patrons. Thus there came into being—no doubt to the stupefaction of St. Francis, had he still been alive—a splendid church that has been called the Westminster Abbey of Florence, so full is it of monuments and tombs of the famous. Among those commemorated there are Michelangelo, the poet and patriot Vittorio Aflieri, and the humanist and historian Leonardo Bruni. The name Santa Croce was particularly relevant to the life of St. Francis, for he showed intense veneration for the Cross on which the Savior had died. Indeed, it was while he was contemplating the Cross and meditating on the Passion that he is said to have received the stigmata.

Throughout the second half of the thirteenth century the rivalry between the old nobility and the new mercantile class intensified. By 1289 the latter felt themselves sufficiently powerful to decree the freeing of the serfs still employed on estates in remoter country areas; and, by 1293, to promulgate the Ordinamenti della Giustizia, or the Ordinances of Justice. These stipulated that no nobleman could take part in the government unless he first renounced his rank and became a member of one of the Greater Guilds. In addition, since the nobility were perpetually causing civil disturbances, each member had to swear an oath of good conduct and deposit a sum of ten thousand librae as a bond.

The moving spirit behind this legislation was a kind of Florentine Philippe Egalité, Giano della Bella, a nobleman who served as prior in 1292. He is said to have had a personal reason for his enmity toward his own class, commencing during a dispute with another nobleman, Berto Frescobaldi, who grabbed him by the nose and threatened to cut it off. As a result of his ordinances Bella, like many another reformer, earned as much unpopularity as popularity. He was accused of using the ordinances merely as a way to get back at his enemies, and one disgusted nobleman declared that he dared not even let his horse whisk its tail in front of a *popolano* for fear of having to forfeit his bond.

In 1295, as Bella was planning further reforms, a revolt—largely engineered by Dante's kinsman by marriage Corso Donati—toppled him from office. His possessions confiscated, he had to leave Florence and take up residence in Paris, where he soon died. The burgher class, or *popolo grasso*, saw this event as its chance to join with the nobility and seize the reins of government. They did not dare to defy the will of the people to the extent of repealing the ordinances, but they did modify the clause which stated that the only people eligible to be priors were guildsmen who actively practiced their profession. Now it was enough merely to be on the roll of a guild; and it was thus that the patrician Dante, by

gaining admission to one of the Greater Guilds, that of Doctors and Apothecaries, was able to take office under the Republic.

Now that the Ghibellines had been virtually eradicated, a split appeared among the Guelphs. As so often occurs in such cases, the reason was in part one of principle and in part one of personalities. The political divergence was over the advisability of attempting to repeal the ordinances; the personal one, over a rivalry between the ancient house of Donati, headed by Corso Donati, and the newly rich Cerchi family. An existing feud had intensified after the Florentines intervened in the repeated clashes between rival wings of the Cancellieri family—the "White" Cancellieri and the "Black" Cancellieri—in neighboring Pistoia. Having stopped the fighting, the soldiers of the Republic brought the leading belligerents away with them to Florence, lodging those who were "White" with the Cerchi, and those who were "Black" with the Frescobaldi, who were fierce adherents of the Donati cause. Hosts took sides with guests, with the result that the Cerchi and their allies became "White"; the Frescobaldi, Donati, and their allies, "Black."

At the height of the conflict, with the government of the priors proving less and less successful in maintaining even a semblance of order, Pope Boniface VIII made an ill-advised attempt at intervention. Not the first or last successor of the Apostle Peter to dream of world domination for his Church, he decided that the acquisition of Tuscany could be the first step on this road; and since the Donati and their adherents were more sympathetic to papal power—the Cerchi and their allies being more sympathetic to the absent emperor—it was to the former that he looked for support. He therefore dispatched Cardinal Matteo d'Acquasparta as his new envoy, ostensibly to make impartial peace but in fact to do what he could to help the "Blacks," who were now in a state of considerable disarray, their leader, Corso Donati, having been banished for flagrantly attempting to tamper with justice. The cardinal's mission failed, since the priors obstinately refused to accept his jurisdiction; and so, having put Florence under an interdict, he returned to Rome.

Corso Donati soon arrived there too, and through his influence with the papal bankers he prevailed on the pope to intervene again, this time more decisively. Boniface dispatched his old papal lieutenant Charles of Valois, who entered Florence on All Saints Day in 1303. Like the cardinal before him, his nominal role was that of peacemaker but his true object was nothing less than removing the "Whites" from power and putting the "Blacks" in their place. In the Church of Santa Maria Novella he took an oath to do all in his ability to maintain peace between the two opposing factions. Then—"jousting with the lance of Judas," as Dante put it—he promptly armed his followers so that they could keep the "Whites" in check while Corso Donati and his adherents sacked and, in many cases, burned their houses. This done, Charles expelled the "White" members of the Signoria, replacing them with "Blacks," and then appointed a new *podestà*, Cante de' Gabrielli, who could carry out his policies.

It was these events that led to the expulsion of

La sposa—"*the bride*"—*was Michelangelo's nickname for the great Dominican basilica of Santa Maria Novella, his way of suggesting the radiant innocence of this supreme example of Tuscan Gothic architecture. Designed by Dominicans in 1246 and dedicated to the education of the young—Cimabue and Dante among them—Santa Maria Novella was also decorated by Dominicans. Fra Filippo Lippi's frescoes for the Strozzi Chapel reveal this immensely gifted cleric working in an unusually theatrical vein, perhaps inspired by the masques that were so popular in Renaissance Florence. The famous Spanish Chapel, part of the cloisters of Santa Maria Novella, is the handiwork of the fourteenth-century painter Andrea di Bonaiuto, also known as Andrea da Firenze. His frescoes for the chapel include scenes from the Old Testament (far left) as well as the Life of Christ (above). Appropriate to the order most closely associated with the Inquisition is the panel at near left, whose lower half is "The Church Militant."*

Dante from his native city. He had sided with the "Whites"—who had come, by a strange reversal, to be regarded as Ghibellines despite the fact that they were more democratic than the "Blacks"—and because of this, a plot was hatched against him. He was wrongly accused of peculation during his term of office as prior; was sentenced in absentia to pay a fine of five hundred lire; and then was sentenced, again in absentia, to be burned alive: "*Igne comburatur sic quod moriatur.*" Wandering about Italy for the rest of his days, *pellagrino quasi mendicando*—"a pilgrim, almost a beggar"—the greatest of Italian poets was never able to return to his native city or again set eyes on his wife. His house in Via Santa Margherita was sacked by order of the authorities.

Despite these internecine squabblings throughout the thirteenth century, however, the city grew apace. Before the year 1400, in fact, two of the most important Florentine buildings had already been raised. One was the Palazzo Vecchio, seat of the Signoria, of which mention has already been made. The other was the Duomo, or cathedral, first known as Santa Maria del Fiore—the "*Fiore,*" or flower, being, of course, the Florentine lily. Built under the supervision of Arnolfo di Cambio between 1294 and 1302—Francesco Talenti, Giovanni di Lapo Ghini, Filippo Brunelleschi, and others were to make subsequent additions and alterations—the edifice takes the form of a Latin cross, with a great nave, two smaller side aisles, two transepts, and two tribunes, out of which open five chapels. Here rest the ashes of St. Zenobius; and, in front of the altar, is Lorenzo Ghiberti's beautiful relief celebrating one of the

miracles performed by this saint, the raising from the dead of a French youth. Here, too, are the tombs of Giotto; of Brunelleschi; of the valiant Bishop Antonio d'Orso, who donned full armor and led his cannons into battle when Henry VII was besieging Florence in 1312; and of Antonio Squarcialupo, "Antonio of the Organs," whose instruments were the delight of Lorenzo de' Medici.

Behind the high altar rises the unfinished group of statuary, the *Pietà*, that is Michelangelo's last work. He would labor over it in his Roman studio far into the night, and it was thus that Vasari found him when the pope sent him to see what progress the sculptor was making. That this curiosity should not be satisfied, Michelangelo pretended to drop the lantern by which he had been working, remarking on the infirmity of extreme old age: "I am so old that death often pulls me by the coat to come with him, and some day I shall fall down like this lantern, and my last spark of life will be extinguished."

While this splendid church was being erected, the young Dante often sat on a stone seat on the south side and watched the builders. The same seat—known as the Sasso di Dante—was still there in 1837, when William Wordsworth, visiting Florence, sat on it too. Later, the English poet commemorated the occasion in one of his less happy sonnets, boasting that he, too, had "for a moment filled that empty Throne." Unhappily, we cannot even for a moment fill that empty Throne ourselves, for it has vanished and only a small slab, set into the wall of a house next to the Palazzo de' Canonici and scarcely noticeable, reminds us that once it was there.

IV

"So sweet a dwelling-place"

Tradition has it that Florence was first walled in by Charlemagne—in an area contained by the Borgo dei Greci, the Badia, the Canto dei Pazzi, Via dei Servi, Borgo San Lorenzo, San Gaetano, and the Porta Rossa (see map, page 164). This small space sufficed until 1077, when a second circuit was made to protect the expanding city from the threatened invasion of Henry IV, then in conflict with Pope Gregory VII and his staunch Tuscan ally, Countess Matilda. The new radius was defined by the Porta Pinti, Piazza Santa Croce, the Lung'Arno, and the Via del Moro. That, during the first third of the fourteenth century, the Florentines should have embarked on a third ring of walls is indicative of two things: first, that the city was growing with amazing rapidity; and second, that there were constant threats of attack from without.

One such threat came from the former Count of Luxembourg, elected to the imperial throne in 1309 as Henry VII. Not realizing that any attempt to reimpose a feudal system on a variety of free, thriving communes would be viewed, at this late date, only as anachronistic and untenable, he mounted an expedition into Italy. For once, the pope, in the person of Clement V, lent his support. Having fallen totally under the domination of the French king, Clement sided with his enemies in the hope that, with the restoration of the empire in Italy, a restoration of his own authority might also come about. All the Guelph cities, previously hostile to emperor after emperor, followed the pope in enthusiastically welcoming Henry VII wherever he appeared. The lone exception was Florence. And the result of this in-

transigence was that, in September of 1312, the imperial army put the city to siege.

At first the outlook was ominous, but with the coming of the rains of autumn the foreign soldiers succumbed to a variety of maladies. (In addition, food supplies grew short.) When the previously strong emperor also sickened with malaria and came near to death, he prudently withdrew his forces to Pisa, there to decide his future tactics.

Surprisingly, when Henry had recovered his health and augmented and reequipped his army, he did not turn immediately toward Florence but instead moved south, in a bid to conquer the Kingdom of Naples. His malaria soon recurred, however, and in August 1313 he died in the little village of Buonconvento. The exiled Dante, ever on the lookout for a leader capable of regenerating and unifying Italy, had mistakenly imagined that this honorable, courageous dreamer of impossible dreams could fill such a role. He had greeted Henry's arrival in Italy with joy and had followed his erratic progress with palpitating interest—and now that the emperor's losing game had been played out to the end, he felt the keenest disappointment.

Within a year Florence had to face another military threat, this one coming when Uguccione della Faggiuola, one of the dead emperor's trusted lieutenants, declared war on the Tuscan Guelphs, captured Lucca, and then won a notable victory against the Florentine forces at Montecatini near Pistoia. A reprieve seemed to have come when Uguccione was unseated by one of his own lieutenants, Castruccio Castracane; but instead of causing this resourceful

and cool-headed young nobleman from Lucca to abandon hostilities, such a reversal only led him to intensify them.

When the threat of invasion by Henry VII was at its height, the Florentines had prudently entered into an agreement with his enemy, Robert, king of Naples. In return for his protection, they agreed to yield him lordship of their city for a period of five years, together with the right to appoint the *podestà*. At the end of the five years, they dithered about renewing the agreement and finally decided that, despite the threat posed by Castruccio, they preferred a dangerous freedom to a safe vassaldom. By this time, Florentine merchants were rarely disposed to serve as soldiers themselves, with the result that the custom of employing foreign mercenaries had become common. It was, therefore, an assortment of French, German, Spanish, and English soldiers who joined the Florentines under a Spanish commander, Raymond of Cardona, to meet the threat posed by Castruccio.

Against this motley opposition, Castruccio won a notable victory at Altopascio in 1325, capturing not merely thousands of soliders but also—an even greater humiliation—the Caroccio. For months thereafter he continued to harrass the Florentines, until, despairing of their ability to evict him from their territories, they once again bartered their independence for a foreigner's protection. In this case, the alien lord was Charles, Duke of Calabria, King Robert's son and heir—who accepted the Signoria, or lordship, on terms even harsher than those exacted by his father. Charles was to be regent for ten

years, was to receive 200,000 florins per annum, and was to enjoy the right of appointing not merely the *podestà* but also the priors and all other officials. In short, he was to become the despot of Florence. But just as death had saved the Florentines, at the last moment, from Henry VII, so it now saved them first from Castruccio, who succumbed to a fever in 1330, and then from the protector they no longer needed, who likewise died of a fever a few months later.

The Florentines suddenly found themselves in the happy position of being able to revert at once to a democratic system of government. They also moved from defense to offense and embarked on a plan to conquer their neighbor and deadly rival, Lucca. When they met with no success in this endeavor, they decided as a last resort to employ a military adventurer—Count Walter of Brienne, who was called the Duke of Athens.

There was, as it happened, a commercial as well as a military reason for calling on this not particularly sagacious outsider to supervise Florentine affairs. By the beginning of the thirteenth century the Florentines had become the chief bankers of Europe, on the one hand lending money to the English kings Henry III and Edward I, and on the other hand collecting the tribute called "St. Peter's Pence" for the Holy See. A single, extremely powerful family of bankers, the Bardi, had representatives in France, England, Ireland, and Germany at this time; and another family, the Frescobaldi, was called upon, through its agent in London, to supervise the whole English banking system under Edward I. It was, no doubt, this commercial supremacy that made Pope

Boniface VIII remark that Florence was "far and away the greatest of all cities. She feeds, clothes and governs us all. Indeed, she appears to rule the whole world. She and her people are, in truth, the fifth element of the universe." Some of this may be discounted as flattery, but it is significant that, at the Papal Jubilee in 1300, no less than twelve powers, including the rulers of France, Germany, and England, were represented by Florentines.

But in 1339 disaster had come. After determinedly expanding their commercial operations at greater and greater risk, many leading Florentine banking houses found themselves suddenly faced with ruin. England's Edward III, engaged in a costly war against the French, had reneged on his debts, and the king of Naples had done likewise. There was the inevitable run on the banks and the government had been obliged to impose a moratorium. As always in a grave economic crisis, revolution threatened—and under the circumstances the *grandi* saw Walter of Brienne not merely as an aggressor against foes without but as a protector against foes within.

Unfortunately, in neither of these roles did the Duke of Athens come up to expectations. He achieved some military successes but little in the way of a decisive victory against Lucca; and, like many another dictator raised to supreme office by a beleaguered ruling class, he soon proved as much of an oppressor to them as to their political opponents. In no time at all he had evicted the *gonfalonier* and priors, suspended the constitution, and taken to himself all power in the city. Eventually, this despotism became so hateful to rich and poor, to *grandi*

and *popolani* alike, that, forgetting all previous differences between them, they combined to evict him. Under siege in the Palazzo Vecchio, the duke made a dishonorable attempt to placate the hostile mob by pushing out, through the palazzo gates, his unpopular chief of police and the chief's eighteen-year-old son. The fourteenth-century historian Villani continues the story: "In the presence of the father and for his greater sorrow, they first dismembered the son, cutting him into tiny pieces; and this done, they did the same to the father." To universal execration, the duke himself was expelled.

In November 1333, Florence suffered a flood, the circumstances of which were to be uncannily duplicated in our own day. Villani describes the ominous beginning as follows:

> At the Ognissanti commenced the rain for Florence and all the surrounding country, and on the Alps, and the mountains; and this continued four days and four nights, the rain increasing in an unusual manner, so that the cataracts of the sky appeared to have been opened, and the lightning fell sufficiently often. Therefore all the people lived in great fear, ringing continuously the bells of the city, so that the water might not rise; and in each house basins and buckets were used, and great cries circulated to God for those in peril, the inmates of the houses fleeing from roof to roof, making bridges of the buildings; and the noise and tumult were so loud that the sound of the thunder was scarcely audible.

A huge wave, which had already destroyed many human beings and animals in the Upper Valdarno,

68

eventually poured over the city. In the Duomo, the water rose above the altar. It covered the steps of the Palazzo Vecchio, left only two piles of the Ponte Vecchio standing in the middle of the Arno, and swept the statue of Mars into the river. When the floods finally retreated, according to Villani, they "left all the city and all the shops and all the cellars—of which there are many in Florence—full of pestilential mud, such as could not be removed for six months.

Robert, king of Sicily, was moved to write a letter to the afflicted city. Quoting from Solomon, Daniel, and St. Augustine, he reminded the Florentines that God sends such tribulations as a sign of his wrath and as an instrument of chastisement. Whether the Florentines took heart from this pious homily, as they viewed their devastated homes, is not recorded.

Fifteen years later, in 1348, the city was to suffer a disaster even more terrible—an epidemic of bubonic plague, the Black Death. Brought to the port of Messina in Sicily by a ship from the East, the plague soon spread over the whole of Europe. It rarely spared its victims, with the result that whole villages would be wiped out—and the dead left unburied. Those who were able to do so—like the survivors who tell their tales in Boccaccio's contemporaneous *Decameron*—retreated to the countryside, where they shut themselves up in their houses and painted the word *Sanitas*—"good health"—on their doors, as though in hiding from some assassin stalking the world in search of them. Although there are no reliable statistics for Florence, it has been estimated that from half to two thirds of its population died.

It is not fanciful to attribute, in part at least, the dawning of the Renaissance to this universal catastrophe. People subjected to so much suffering could not believe—as King Robert had urged them to believe in the case of the floods—that God was exacting punishment for their transgressions. If that were the case, why should the just and the unjust die in equal agony? And why was it that God's anointed servants, whether saintly monks or mighty prelates, should not be immune? Certainly people had asked such questions before, just as they continue to ask them today, but the hideous circumstances of the plague made them cruelly insistent. Thus, perforce, the whole religious basis of life came under scrutiny—and a struggle began to develop between the old Christian dogmas and a new awareness that man is a free agent, with a right to express his thoughts in his own fashion.

Of the three prime movers of the Renaissance, one, Dante Alighieri (1265–1321), was born in Florence; one, Giovanni Boccaccio (1313–1375), was born in Certaldo but spent most of his life in Florence; and one, Francesco Petrarch (1304–1374), came from a Florentine family, although he was born in Arezzo and lived chiefly in France and Rome. But we must look to Dante's mentor, the Florentine Brunetto Latini—whose friendship and counsel the poet repaid in extraordinary fashion by placing him in the seventh circle of Hell, merely for being homosexual—for perhaps the most succinct expression of the Renaissance spirit: "Heaven and earth," Latini wrote, "are made for man, but man is made for himself."

In his magisterial Renaissance in Italy *the perceptive nineteenth-century scholar and critic John Addington Symonds wrote of Petrarch that the foremost historian of the fourteenth century "recognised the dignity of man as a rational being apart from theological determination, and thought that classical literature alone displayed human nature in the plenitude of intellectual and moral freedom." Symonds' assessment of Petrarch, whose robed figure appears at near left, is entirely apt—but it also happens to fit two other giants of the Renaissance, Giovanni Boccaccio (far left) and Dante Alighieri (left, below), with uncanny accuracy. Both of these Florentine writers turned to classical literature for inspiration— Boccaccio to Aesop, Dante to Vergil—and both found in those classical sources human nature in its plenitude.*

In many ways Dante was a profoundly conservative figure in an age of rapid change. But he prepared the ground for the flowering of the Renaissance both by his rapt exploration of classical mythology for its mystical and psychological secrets and by his insistence that there must be a marriage between Christian ideals and Greek and Latin learning. Petrarch, for his part, worshipped Cicero, collected classical coins, manuscripts, and inscriptions, waged war against tradition, pedantry, and superstition, and pleaded for total freedom for the intellect.

Boccaccio began by revering the Roman poet Vergil and Dante in equal measure. Although he was only eight when Dante died, he grew up with an instinctive love of him, calling him his "father," copying out with his own hand the whole of *The Divine Comedy*, and urging Petrarch to study his writings. In 1350, Boccaccio was one of the captains of the *Laudesi*, a confraternity founded to sing the praises of the miraculous Madonna of Or San Michele. The archives of the *Laudesi* contain an entry to the effect that ten gold florins should be handed over to Boccaccio, that he might convey them to "sister Beatrice, daughter of Dante Alighieri, a nun in the monastery of St. Stephen of the Olives in Ravenna." It was, no doubt, his meeting with Dante's daughter and his sight of Dante's tomb on the shores of the Adriatic that spurred Boccaccio to undertake his *Life of Dante*, without which our knowledge of the poet would be far more meager. (In this biography he makes his famous reference to the Florentines as *quell' ingrato popolo maligno*— "that ungrateful and malignant mob"—who drove their greatest son into

exile.) If Petrarch was the pioneer of Latin studies, Boccaccio was of Greek, making a translation of Homer that was to become one of the foundation stones of a revival of Greek literature after some seven hundred years of neglect.

Yet despite the soaring aspirations to intellectual freedom represented by this trio, the Inquisition in Florence, as everywhere else, was brutally quick during these years both to impose orthodoxy and check heresy. It was in the Franciscan church of Santa Croce that the Inquisition maintained its Tribunal and Council Chamber from 1254 to 1782; and it was in the piazza outside this same church that the Inquisitor would mount a pulpit and read out the convictions, after which heretical books and heretics alike would be consigned to the flames while a wondering crowd looked on. In the Spanish Chapel of Santa Maria Novella, Andrea di Bonaiuto, Simone Memmi, and others painted a fresco showing Dominican members of the most militant orders in the form of black and white dogs (*Domini-cani*, or dogs of the Lord) devouring brown wolves that represent the heretics—so that the latter could not prey on the lambs of the fold.

After the explusion of Walter of Brienne in 1339, another struggle for power ensued, this time between the great merchants, represented by such families as the Albizzi and Bardi, and the common folk, who, after the despot's departure, felt themselves cheated of the share in government they had expected him to win for them. Things came to a head in 1378, with the revolt of the *ciompi*—a word, derived from the Italian *compare* and meaning "comrade," which the wool workers applied to each other. Despite their importance to the economy of the city, these men lived in near-destitution and were forbidden to organize themselves into a guild. A month previous to their uprising, which took place in July, there had been another, one in which the *gonfalonier* of the time, Salvestro de' Medici, had taken the side of the minor craftsmen against his own class, the merchant oligarchy. In that rising many merchants had had their houses and shops sacked and had been obliged to flee the city.

By July, Salvestro de' Medici was no longer in office, but the disturbance smouldered on, with the *ciompi* now loudest in proclaiming their grievances. Led by a young wool-comber named Michele di Lando, they eventually stormed the Palazzo Vecchio, which had been hurriedly vacated by the terrified priors, who promptly gave in to the *ciompi's* demands. But, as so often happens when a revolution has succeeded in its first moderate aims, the insurgents refused to be satisfied and, as day succeeded day, they became increasingly extravagant in calling for one concession after another.

By this time Michele di Lando had been appointed *gonfalonier* of the city and, the ardor of his former colleagues now proving too much for him to stomach, he mounted a horse and, with two of his closest associates, rode through the streets exhorting the citizens to join him in putting an end to the insurrection. His cry of "Long live the trade guilds and the people, death to traitors who would bring foreign lords to rule the city!" met with so enthusiastic a response that peace was soon restored. In return

for his having saved the city almost single-handedly, the grateful Signoria presented him with a horse and the shield and pennon of knighthood; and, since it was not fitting that a former *gonfalonier* should return to his mother's little greengrocer's shop, he was made *podestà* of Barberino. After this brief interregnum of populist rule, the merchant oligarchy once again asserted an authority it was not to lose until Florence was absorbed into a united Italy five hundred years later.

Despite the floods, the Black Death, wars, and internal dissension, the fourteenth century was one in which great buildings were raised in Florence and great works of art completed. Mention has already been made of the Duomo, Santa Croce, and the Palazzo Vecchio, all erected in the first third of the century. Giotto, who was appointed master builder of the Duomo in 1332, received instructions from the Signoria in 1334 that he should erect a campanile which, in grandeur and richness, should surpass all other towers, ancient and modern. This prescription he fulfilled triumphantly, producing what Elizabeth Barrett Browning justifiably called "The lily of Florence blossoming in stone." Without the aid of buttresses, the airy building, pierced by large Italian Gothic windows, rises to a height of 276 feet. Nothing seems to support it but its corner pilasters; nothing to bind it together but its string-courses.

Giotto came late to architecture, having spent a long life creating not merely such works in Florence as his *Life of St. John the Baptist* in the Peruzzi Chapel of Santa Croce and his *Life of St. Francis* in the Bardi Chapel of the same church, but a beautiful series of

No church in all of Florence has quite as unusual and intriguing a history as Or San Michele, a transitional Gothic-Renaissance structure that was erected in the thirteenth century as a grain market. When a flash fire destroyed this loggia, a second—half market, half church—was constructed. In time, the entire building was given over to worship and the grain merchants moved elsewhere. They left their mark, however—in the form of their guild's coat of arms, affixed to an exterior pilaster—and so did dozens of other arti, *or commercial guilds. The roof-support at right honors the Guild of Farriers, as the association of blacksmiths was known.*

biblical stories in the Convent of Santa Chiara, near Naples, and of course his incomparable frescoes in the Church of St. Francis at Assisi. Vasari said of Giotto that "He translated art from Greek into Italian." For Greek, we must here read Byzantine—and what Vasari meant was that Giotto had taken a dead artistic language and transmuted it into a living one. How he did this we can at once observe if we look into the eyes of one of his figures. They are Oriental in their almond shape, as in the icons of the Byzantine masters, but there is this difference: they are full of life and expression. When Giotto executed a portrait, he showed a perception of character rare at that time. Thus we are instantly aware that his Pope Boniface VII is a worldly, cunning, and formidable figure, and that his Dante is a far-seeing visionary.

Giotto was the first Italian painter to translate biblical life into the ordinary simplicities to be seen in any Italian city of his time. Dressed in the clothes of the period, his figures are Italians—not the inhabitants of some country remote in geography and time—acting out the familiar stories of the Bible; and they do so, not against the gold background of the icons, but against Italian buildings and Italian landscapes such as can still be seen in Tuscany.

A building of this period almost as remarkable as Giotto's campanile is the church of Or San Michele. On its site there originally stood a small chapel that bore the name San Michele in Orto, or St. Michael in the Garden. In the middle of the thirteenth century this chapel was cleared away to make room for a grain market, an open loggia of brick. Although this was otherwise a secular building, it nonetheless re-

tained on one of its piers a picture of the Madonna and Child that was believed to be the work of a primitive painter, Ugolino de Siena. Interestingly, this picture can be glimpsed in its original position in an old manuscript in the Laurentian Library in Florence. Below, the Clerk of the Market is depicted, busy with his accounts, and buyers and sellers jostle each other. Above their heads the Madonna can be seen in her little shrine.

The fame of this Madonna, believed to possess miraculous powers, eventually spread through the whole of Tuscany, with pilgrims coming long distances to bring their votive offerings and make their petitions. Guido Cavalcanti, the great thirteenth-century poet and friend of Dante, refers in a sonnet, with what seems to be a smiling irony, to the wonders wrought by this image in exorcising demons, giving sight to the blind, and healing the sick. In 1303, during one of those brawls between noble houses so common at the time, the loggia caught fire and burned to the ground. The miraculous Madonna was saved, however, and in 1336 another loggia, now half grain market and half church, was begun under the supervision of Francesco Talenti, Neri di Fioravante, and Benci di Cione, all of whom were also engaged in the building of the cathedral. Forty years later, the whole building became a church when the open arcades of the market were filled with tracery and turned into windows.

One of the chief interests of the present Or San Michele is that the adornment of its exterior was handed over to the *Arti*. Each guild stipulated that the pilasters supporting the roof should be decorat-

ed with the image of its patron saint and its coat of arms, with the result that we have, graven in stone, a record of all the guilds that played such an important part in the history of the city.

It was during this century that the Ponte alla Carraia was twice rebuilt, only to be swept away each time by flood. The original bridge, made of wood, had been erected in 1218 to accommodate an increase in traffic caused by the growth of the wool and silk industry in the area it served, Borgo Ognissanti. In 1304, a dense crowd assembled on it to watch a mystery play enacted on boats in the river, and the bridge collapsed beneath their weight, drowning many of the spectators. By a grim irony, the work being presented was entitled "Inferno."

From Roman times the Ponte Vecchio had, in one form or another, spanned what Dante alternately called *il bel fiume*—"the beautiful river"—and *la maladetta e sventurata fossa*—"the cursed and luckless ditch." But "the old treasure bridge, most precious historical link of all, tottering under the weight of shops and galleries," as Ruskin called it, had to be rebuilt in 1345, after the floods. Tradition has it that the architect on this occasion was Giotto's godson, Taddeo Gaddi, who, like Giotto himself, had first made his name as a painter of frescoes.

In addition to these public works the *grandi* built themselves magnificent private dwellings, vying with each other in the splendor of their houses just as once they had vied with each other in the height of their towers. The most interesting of those that still survive is the Palazzo Davanzati, which has been restored to precisely the same condition in which Pope Eugenius IV found it when he lodged there in 1434. His hosts then were the Davizza family. The Davanzati bought it late in the sixteenth century and remained its owners until the mid-nineteenth century. In 1904 it passed into the hands of Professor Elia Volpi, who first lovingly restored it and then presented it to the city. As one goes around it, one can only feel, as at Elsinore in Denmark, that even for the rich and privileged daily life in earlier centuries must have been extremely uncomfortable. The furniture is unupholstered; the rooms are too vast to be adequately warmed by the single smoky fire; and all water must have been obtained by dipping down into the same dank, unhygienic shaft.

If the lives of the *grandi* have changed greatly since that time, those of the poor of Florence have remained remarkably the same. Many of those who live in the city still lack running water, and many still lower baskets out of the windows of their high-rise apartments so that the deliverers of produce can put goods into them. Over the centuries, people have gone to the same shops to the get their shoes mended, to buy their groceries, or to outfit their children; to the same tap-rooms to drink and to the same *trattorie* to eat; to the same churches to be married and to have their offspring baptized and parents buried.

Seeing this unchanging life in the midst of so much change, one can only echo Dante's words:

Così bello viver di cittandini . . . a così dolce ostello.
So fine a life of citizens . . . in so sweet a dwelling-place.

The guidebooks tell you what to see if you have two days in Florence, or three, or more. They list palaces and public squares, museums and churches, statues and gardens. What they do not list is the unexpected pleasures and unassertive delights ,of Florence's back streets and byways—a letter-drop of time-worn marble, a curlicue of wrought iron, an ivy-walled aerie for two. These, too, are part of the city's remarkable heritage, unanticipated but unforgettable.

V

Pater Patriae

The fifteenth century marked the apogee of the greatness of Florence. During it, this city, small by modern standards, can truthfully be said to have become the commercial, intellectual, and artistic capital of Europe. Only fifth-century B.C. Athens can boast a comparable achievement—a fact recognized by the poet Shelley when he apostrophized Florence in these times in "Marenghi":

> O! Foster-nurse of man's abandoned glory
> Since Athens, its great mother, sunk in
> —splendour . . .

The century began with Florence already embroiled in intermittent conflict with a number of her neighbors, the most powerful of which were Milan, Pisa, Lucca, Siena, and Naples. That it survived all attempts to encroach on its territory and, in 1405, even succeeded in defeating and annexing Pisa, was due, in part, to the brilliance of the *condottieri* it employed to lead its armies. It was also due, in part, to the skill with which it played off one enemy against another through a series of exceptionally cunning diplomatic maneuvers. The preservation of the balance of power, so often regarded as an invention of nineteenth-century British diplomacy, was in fact already being practiced by the Florentines with extreme subtlety and ruthlessness at this early date.

The dominant Florentine family during the first quarter of the fifteenth century was the Albizzi, led by Maso degli Albizzi, in partnership with the heads of two other merchant dynasties, Gino Capponi and Niccolò da Uzzano. With this faction, the rising family of Medici found itself increasingly in conflict.

The founder of this house, which was to play an even more dominant role in the history of Florence than the Cecils in that of Britain, was Giovanni di Averardo, also called Giovanni di Bicci (1368–1429). Head of a bank with the motto *Col nome di Dio e di bona ventura*—"With the name of God and of good luck"—this astute businessman, a kind of fifteenth-century Joseph Kennedy, received sufficient help from both these sources to amass vast sums of money—without which his descendants would have been unlikely to achieve supreme political power.

Giovanni seems to have had only faint political ambitions, although in 1421 he did take office as *gonfalonier*, but clearly he was a man of considerable influence, having been appointed one of the judges in the competition to pick a designer of a new set of Baptistry doors in 1401. The winner of this competition, Lorenzo Ghiberti, has himself given an account of all the particulars. Each of the artists involved— Filippo Brunelleschi was his chief rival—was given a bronze plate of a certain size and was told to bring back, within a year, his version of "The Offering of Isaac." Ghiberti's and Brunelleschi's reliefs can now be seen side by side in the Bargello and it is easy to understand the judges' preference for Ghiberti's, which is both technically superior and aesthetically more appealing.

When Giovanni died in 1429, he left one son, Cosimo, aged forty, and a second, Lorenzo, aged thirty-four; and it was only then that the rivalry between the Medici on the one hand and the Albizzi and their allies on the other resulted in an open breach. By this time Maso degli Albizzi was also dead and the

leadership of the Albizzi faction had passed to his son Rinaldo, who had none of the prudence or sagacity of either his father or his father's old crony Niccolò da Uzzano. In 1429, Rinaldo, who was virtual ruler of the city, decided on yet another war against Lucca. In this he had, surprisingly, the support of Cosimo de' Medici, who even consented to serve on the Board of War. Hostilities dragged on for four years, with no result other than a depletion of Florentine resources and a considerable loss of life, and in 1433 Rinaldo opted for peace.

Humiliated, the Florentines turned against him and proposed to replace him with Cosimo—who, although he had ostensibly supported the war, had nonetheless let word go around that he was less than enthusiastic about Rinaldo's conduct of it. Sensing that if he did not take some immediate action he might be unseated, Rinaldo, always reckless, gave orders for the arrest of Cosimo in his country villa in the Mugello hills, where the Medici had originated. He was to be incarcerated in the tower cell in the Palazzo Vecchio, and eventually put on trial. For a few days Cosimo was confined to the tower cell, where he lived in constant dread of execution—which lifted when he was sent into exile in Venice with his brother (according to some accounts because he had arranged for large bribes to be paid to those most hostile to him). However, the removal of his rival did not save Rinaldo, who found the protests against his rule becoming even more vociferous. Despite the intervention of Pope Eugene IV, who had taken up residence in the monastery of Santa Maria Novella after being driven out of Rome

by an uprising, the fickle Signoria soon recalled Cosimo and banished Rinaldo. In 1434 Cosimo took over supreme rule. It was not to leave his hands until his death thirty years later.

In accordance with the family motto, both God and fortune seemed to smile on Cosimo in his moment of accession. God's representative, Pope Eugene, was to remain a resident of the city for almost ten years, with the result that for that time Rome was replaced by Florence as the capital of Christendom. Luck had seen to it that one of the marvels of the age, Brunelleschi's vast dome of the Cathedral of Santa Maria del Fiore, had just approached completion, and Cosimo, astute as always, at once seized the opportunity to bring pope and dome together, in a magnificent ceremony of consecration—on the Feast of the Annunciation, March 25, 1436.

The story is told by Vasari of how Brunelleschi, a man of indisputable genius and of no less indisputable pettiness and selfishness, fought first to persuade the officials of the Opera del Duomo that his plan was a feasible way of roofing over the central part of the church and then fought to make sure that Ghiberti, his successful rival for the commission of the Bapistery doors, should have no share of the credit for the architectural miracle.

Brunelleschi had shown such extraordinary pertinacity and thoroughness—inspecting the clay for the bricks and then the bricks themselves, providing models for the iron girders, for the wooden supports, and for the shaping of each stone—that it was not without reason that the Signoria should have described him in a proclamation as *vir perspicassimi in-*

Florence at the end of the thirteenth century was a city of growing commercial and political importance—and welling civic pride. Santa Reparata, the cathedral deemed sufficient at the time of Dante's birth in 1265, was now held to be "crudely built and too small for such a city." Such a city as Florence had become plainly needed a new cathedral, one to rival those at Siena and Pisa, one which would, in the words of the Signoria, "possess the utmost and most sumptuous magnificence." With this hyperbolic mandate as his guide, the master architect Arnolfo di Cambio conceived an enormous new cathedral rising, according to the French model, from cloverleaf-shaped foundations (above). Arnolfo, who died in 1302, just as those foundations were being laid and the courses rising upon them, did not live to see his plans brought to fruition, but then no one involved in planning the Duomo did. Some 175 years were to pass between the laying of the cornerstone and the sheathing of the exterior in multicolored marble (right), and in that time the cost was to rise to 18 million gold florins.

tellecti et industriae et inventionis admirabilis—"a man of the most perspicacious intellect and of admirable industry and invention." However, like many another pioneering genius, he was capable of terrible miscalculations. Thus, in 1430, during the course of yet another war with Lucca, he hit on the brilliant idea of diverting the Serchio River to inundate the enemy camp. Unfortunately, it was the Florentines who were inundated in this case, not the Luccans.

In addition to the loggia of the Ospedale degli Innocenti on the Piazza SS. Annunziata, Brunelleschi busied himself with other important commissions even while he was working on the giant cupola. It is now doubted that he was the architect of the superb Palazzo Lenzi Busini, as was for a long time assumed, but he certainly had a major part in the rebuilding of the Palazzo di Parte Guelfa (now the Università Popolare, a kind of night school) in the Via delle Terme. He also designed the Pazzi Chapel, an octagonal building with a dome, for the chief rivals to the Medici, and he left plans for the Church of S. Spirito. In all these buildings he abandoned what Vasari called the *todesca e barbara*—"barbarous Gothic"—and returned to the pilasters and architraves of Roman architecture—thus setting an example for such gifted contemporaries as Michelozzo Michelozzi and Leon Battista Alberti.

In 1439, three years after the consecration of the cathedral overarched by the wonder of its dome, all Christendom was once again talking of an event in Florence. This was a General Council of the Catholic and Orthodox churches—where, it was hoped, as it has often been hoped since, that an ancient schism could somehow be healed. What drove the Byzantine emperor, John Paleologus, to seek an accommodation with the pope was the threat of the Ottoman Turks, who were drawing a noose tighter and tighter around the city of Constantinople. What persuaded Pope Eugene to choose Florence as their meeting place was his financial inability to support the vast Byzantine delegation, with which he had had a preliminary and expensive encounter in Ferrara. Only the Medici and the commune could, between them, provide the essential funds. Sumptuous lodgings were prepared for the Patriarch of Constantinople in the Palazzo Ferrantini in the Borgo Pinti—where, such was his feebleness and age, he soon fell sick and died. The Peruzzi Palace, the home of a once-rich banking family ruined when Edward III defaulted on a loan, was given over to the emperor and his huge retinue of priests, nobles, and servants. The pope stayed, as before, in the convent attached to Santa Maria Novella. The meetings—as an inscription on one of the piers of the Duomo still records for us today—were held under Brunelleschi's splendid dome. A concordat seemed to have been reached, with the emperor agreeing to the submission of the Eastern Church to Rome in return for the promise of military aid against the Turks; but no sooner had John Paleologus returned to Constantinople than there was such an outcry against the terms to which he had assented that he was obliged at once to repudiate them. From that moment, the doom of Constantinople was certain.

If John Paleologus lost, Cosimo gained, enormously enhancing his stature by playing host to em-
peror, patriarch, and pope at the same time. In addition, a more lasting benefit accrued. Accompanying the patriarch and the emperor were many churchmen and scholars, who brought with them knowledge, ideas, and even actual manuscripts totally unfamiliar in Italy. The foremost of these scholars was George Gemistus Plethon, the legate from Trebizond, whom Cosimo persuaded to make Florence his home so that he could give instructions in Platonism. This handsome and erudite man soon found a ready disciple in Marsilio Ficino, youthful son of Cosimo's physician; and it was Ficino, the translator of Plotinus, who was one of the moving spirits in the founding of the Platonic Academy during the rule of Cosimo's son Lorenzo. In *Renaissance in Italy* John Addington Symonds claims that this Platonic Academy had a tremendous, if subterranean, influence on thought not merely in Italy but, through Johann Reuchlin and his pupil Philipp Melancthon, in Germany and so, eventually, through all the countries of Europe.

Cosimo had already shown himself to be an avid collector of books, sending his agents to make purchases on his behalf all over Europe and the Middle East. Those which even a man of his wealth could not secure, he would have copied—inevitably, before Johann Gutenberg invented his press, at enormous labor and expense. The man who was chiefly responsible, with a team of dedicated scribes and illuminators, for doing this copying was Vespasiano da Bisticci, a remarkable author and bookseller who assisted in the formation not merely of the Laurentian Library in Florence but also the Vatican Library

in Rome. The books that emanated from his studio were works of high art, to which illuminator, calligrapher, binder, and goldsmith all contributed their devoted skills. One such book alone cost more than any ordinary citizen could afford, and during the congress Vespasiano employed forty-five people to copy two hundred codices.

The effect of the new learning from Byzantium was to make people question both the claims of the See of Rome to religious supremacy—the authenticity of documents on which this claim had been based was now put in question—and, more widely, all the previously accepted tenets of Christianity. The doubts about the See of Rome became, in the words of G. F. Young, the greatest historian of the Medici, "a train of powder" that eventually set off the Reformation; the doubts about Christianity itself produced the moral laxity and religious skepticism that, in this same century and city, Savonarola was to assail with so much fervor.

It was in 1444, a year after Pope Eugene was at last able to leave his haven in Florence for Rome, that Cosimo founded the Medici Library. Since it was open to all scholars, it has often been described as the first public library in the world. Initially, it was housed in the monastery of San Marco. Then, as more and more volumes were added to it, it was moved to the Biblioteca Laurentiana, or Laurentian Library, begun by Michelangelo in 1524 at the behest of Pope Clement IV—himself a Medici, although illegitimate by birth. Here can be seen the parchment that records the abortive concordat reached amid so much splendor in the Great Coun-

Never was a painter more fittingly named than was Fra Angelico, whose life and art were both above reproach. A selfless and tireless workman, he was to spend years transforming the Dominican monastery of San Marco into one vast Gospel Book, a sustained hymn to color and to Saint Dominic, founder of the Blessed Angelico's order. The result is, in addition, a psalm to the painter—and a unique trove of his works, among them an Annunciation *that is his acknowledged masterpiece. So taken was Cosimo de Medici with the beauty and serenity of San Marco that he had a cell set aside for himself in the monastery—and then had Fra Angelico adorn it with an* Adoration, *lest he forget the necessity of humility, even among the mighty. At right, a similar* Adoration, *this one the work of Fra Angelico and another talented Dominican, Filippo Lippi.*

cil of 1439. Here, too, are such treasures as the original copy of the sixth-century Pandects of Justinian, the discovery of which, in the twelfth century, had a profound effect on the study of Roman law; a fifth-century Vergil, among other classical texts of inestimable value; and the holograph of the sculptor Cellini's autobiography.

The reconstruction of San Marco was typical of the public works that Cosimo undertook at his own expense. The monastery had originally been built by Vallombrosan monks in the thirteenth century. Silvistrine monks had taken over from them, but after the plague had decimated their number the buildings had fallen into a state of dilapidation and the monks into a state of ill-repute. In 1436, Pope Eugene had ordered Dominicans from the monastery of San Giorgio at San Miniato to take over the buildings, at the same time banishing the Silvistrines to a place more humble. In the following year Cosimo retained Michelozzo Michelozzi to design the new church. After the death of Brunelleschi, Michelozzi had succeeded to his position as the foremost architect of the time. He was also a close friend of Cosimo, whom he had accompanied into Venetian exile in 1433. On their return he had been given the task of repairing Arnolfo's Palazzo Vecchio, some parts of which were no longer safe, and he also designed two of the finest Florentine palazzi, at once rugged and elegant, the Tornabuoni and the Riccardi. After he had completed his work on San Marco, it was Michelozzi who built the magnificent Villa Medici at Careggi and another villa, for Cosimo's son Giovanni, at Fiesole.

The Church and Monastery of San Marco may be regarded as a museum dedicated to Fra Angelico, since the whole interior is like some huge Gospel Book illustrated by him and his helpers, with St. Dominic, founder of the order to which he belonged, pictured on almost every page as *il famigliar di Cristo*, as Dante called him, "the intimate of Christ." Religious painters can be divided into two categories: those whose subjects were religious because that was what was asked of them; and those whose dedication to God was such that they could paint nothing else. It is in this second category that Fra Angelico must be placed. Vasari has recorded how, each time Fra Angelico picked up his brush, he would offer a prayer, and how, each time he depicted Christ on the Cross, he would shed tears. His most famous saying is *Chi fa le cose di Cristo, con Cristo deve star sempre*—"He who does the work of Christ must always live with Christ"—and this was the basic principle of every work he executed. Ruskin's verdict—"The art of Fra Angelico, both in drawing and colouring, is perfect"—may not receive universal assent, since in his depiction of human form he was certainly no anatomist; but Ruskin's other verdict—that Fra Angelico "gives perhaps the best idea of spiritual being which the human is capable of forming"—admits of no argument.

Cosimo had a double-chambered cell set aside for himself in the monastery, where he could retire periodically from the cares and pomp of his worldly life for spiritual rest and recreation. No. 38 in a series—all of which were adorned by Fra Angelico and his followers—Cosimo's cell has on its wall an *Adoration*

89

When Donatello unveiled his magnificent bronze David *in 1432, it created an instantaneous sensation. Among other things, this life-sized work was the first totally freestanding nude figure created since antiquity, and it blended naturalism and classicism in a manner that was at once sensitive and striking. The relaxed pose recalls works by Praxiteles, as does the sensuously modeled adolescent form. Indeed, it is this* David's *body that speaks more directly to the viewer, his rather inexpressive features hidden beneath the wide brim of a shepherd's hat. Michelangelo's renowned treatment of the same subject, completed three quarters of a century later, shares the same quality of arresting physicality but differs in almost every other respect.*

of the Magi. This was at his own request, since he wished to be reminded of the need for all earthly rulers to be subservient to God.

Cosimo also used his immense financial resources to commission first Brunelleschi—outside—and then Antonio Manetti—inside—to rebuild the Church of San Lorenzo on the site of a basilica founded by a Florentine woman, Giuliana, on the birth of her long-awaited son, and consecrated, according to tradition, by no less a personage than St. Ambrose in 393. Another church built to Cosimo's orders is the exquisite La Badia in San Domenico, below Fiesole, commonly attributed to Brunelleschi, although it was not erected until after his death.

Donatello was the sculptor whom Cosimo most favored; *di continuto lo faceva lavorare*—"he continually kept him working"—according to Vasari. It was for Cosimo that Donatello executed what is probably the most famous of his works, his *David*, to stand in the *cortile* of the Medici Palace, and it was at Cosimo's behest that he executed four saints, a wash-basin, and a bronze door, all of superb workmanship, in the Church of San Lorenzo. So great was Cosimo's affection and gratitude that he bequeathed to Donatello a farm in the Mugello region.

Cosimo also looked with favor on Fra Lippo Lippi, pupil of Masaccio, who, though he died young, had a potent influence not merely on Lippi but on many of his contemporaries. Ne'er-do-well son of a butcher and renegade monk, Fra Lippo Lippi was the total antithesis of Fra Angelico in his worldliness, laziness, dissipation, and dishonesty. So reluctant was he to do any work that, when he was engaged on his *Coronation of the Virgin*, now in the Accademia delle Belle Arti, for Cosimo, his tough patron had him locked up in a room with instructions that he was not to be released until the picture was done. Fra Lippo Lippi, resourceful as always, made a rope of his bedclothes, climbed out of the window, and disappeared to the brothels of Florence, not to reappear for several days.

Tradition, often disputed, has it that, while using as his model for the Madonna a novice nun named Lucretia Buti, from the Convent of Santa Margherita, Fra Lippo Lippi agreed to help her and·her sister escape from the life-in-death of a cloistered order, for which they had no vocation. This he succeeded in doing, but there was so great a scandal when Lucretia became pregnant with the child who would eventually be christened Filippino Lippi, that shame drove both her and her sister back into the convent. In time, however, Cosimo was able to obtain from Pope Pius II a dispensation for the two women to leave the convent once again and for Fra Lippo Lippi to marry Lucretia. It has been suggested that what endeared Lippi to Cosimo was precisely his worldliness. It is difficult otherwise to see why, on the one hand, he should so often have extended help to Lippi, and, on the other, should never have patronized either Paolo Uccellò or Andrea del Castagno, even though most people would regard them as greater painters.

No one can doubt that Cosimo had a genuine interest in architecture and art; but, in considering his lavish benefactions, it is essential to remember that in Renaissance Florence, as in the world today, patronage served as an expression of power. Just as a tour of eighteenth-century English country houses becomes a lesson in the history of the period, so a tour of the *palazzi* and private chapels of Renaissance Florence serves the same purpose. In each case, there is no doubt about which families were dominant. Thus, when Cosimo rebuilt San Lorenzo or San Marco, filling them with paintings and sculptures by the greatest artists of his time, he was acting not merely out of artistic or religious fervor but also to make an assertion about his own supremacy. It was fortunate for posterity that, like the aristocrats of eighteenth-century England, the Medici of the Florentine Renaissance were, as a rule, men of impeccable taste.

Cosimo's achievements both as a politician and as a patron of the arts always remained dependent on his astonishing skill and nerve as a banker. It was his vast fortune that gathered round him a close-knit little "family" and kept them loyal to their "godfather," and it was this same fortune, doubled in his lifetime, that he so often used as an instrument of political policy. Did he wish to humiliate the French and their puppet, Filippo Visconti, duke of Milan? Then he made over a huge sum to the Venetians, who were at war with them. Did Venice and Naples enter into an alliance to make war against Florence in 1452? At once he called in his debts from those states, thus reducing them to a condition in which an expensive campaign was out of the question. But for Medici money, it is unlikely that Edward IV of England would have hung onto his throne in the internecine War of the Roses.

The private life of Cosimo is reputed to have been old-fashioned in its simplicity; but the public ceremonials in which he and his family participated—the banquets, the musical and dramatic entertainments, the weddings, the funerals, the jousting tournaments in front of S. Croce—were, like the munificent commissions to artists and architects, a means of proclaiming Medici glory and might to the whole civilized world. Less than a decade after Cosimo's death, his grandson Lorenzo could boast that, since 1434, the Medici had spent over 600,000 florins for public purposes, adding that this generosity "brilliantly illumines our condition in the city."

When Cosimo died in August 1464, at his country villa in Careggi, at the age of seventy-five, the slab over his tomb was inscribed merely *Pater Patriae*—"father of his country." Since he had always treated his fellow citizens as children for whom he knew what was best, the word *Pater* was appropriate. Clearly, few had resented a paternalism so shrewd, efficient, and benevolent.

Cosimo was succeeded by his son Piero. Known as *Il Gottoso*—"the Gouty"—he is now thought to have suffered from a peculiarly painful and disabling form of arthritis. Because of this ailment, he was unable to make frequent public appearances and has therefore tended to be underestimated by historians until recent times. In fact, he was as shrewd a businessman and politician as his father, and as assiduous a patron and scholar. His skill as a politician soon had to be demonstrated, for in 1466 an anti-Medici faction threatened to attack Florence with the help of Venice and some of the minor states of

Romagna. Though confined to his bed in the country, Piero had himself carried into Florence on a litter and there decisively mobilized the pro-Medici forces to deal with the rebels. Three of the ringleaders, Niccolò Soderini, Agnolo Acciaiuoli, and Dietisalvi Neroni, were sent into exile. A fourth, Luca Pitti, then seventy years old and former associate of Cosimo, had already sought pardon and reconciliation and these, magnanimously, Piero granted. At a time when rebellion was punished with death—and often torture before death was inflicted—Piero's restraint was remarkable.

Piero was succeeded in 1469 by his son Lorenzo, known as "the Magnificent" not in his own time but to subsequent generations. Because of Piero's chronic ill-health, Cosimo had given to his grandson, when he was still only an adolescent, every possible opportunity to learn about statecraft. His tutor was Marsilio Ficino, a disciple of George Gemistus Plethon and head of the Platonic Academy. When Piero put down the rebellion against the Medici with so much authority and yet without shedding a single drop of blood, Lorenzo had been at his side, to counsel and support him. To further strengthen Lorenzo's position, a dynastic marriage was arranged for him with Clarice, daughter of the ancient and powerful Roman family of Orsini. Not for the last time, a family of millionaires married off their future head into the aristocracy in the hope of thus obscuring their humble origins.

Ludovico Sforza, usurper of the rule of Milan from his lazy and weak nephew, remarked of Lorenzo that he had converted an inheritance of glass

Never were two brothers less alike than Lorenzo and Giuliano de Medici. Nature, having favored the former with a quick mind, sound judgment, refined sensibilities and uncanny surefootedness in the quagmire of local politics, denied him the ravishing good looks and the radiant health enjoyed by the latter. Looks and health were not enough to ensure Giuliano's survival, however; in 1478 he fell beneath the knives of his enemies in what became known as the Pazzi Conspiracy. Lorenzo's revenge was not particularly swift but it was certainly complete: by 1480 he had established himself as supreme in Florence—"the needle of the Italian compass." The coin opposite, struck to commemorate Lorenzo's triumph, shows his profile on the obverse (near right) and that of the handsome but ill-fated Giuliano on the reverse.

into one of iron. To enable him to do this, fate had endowed him with a multitude of talents. As a youth he had excelled at athletics, and even in his maturity he would often get up, in the worlds of Marsilio Ficino, "when the east is already red and the tops of the mountains appear to be gold" in order to go hunting. He was the most discriminating collector of gems and intaglios, preferring such *objects d'art* to pictures. He was as much absorbed by the consideration of some new idea, presented for his inspection at the Platonic Academy, as by the contemplation of the clock, a miracle of the horologist's art, made for him by Lorenzo da Volpaja, to show not merely the hours of the day but the motions of the sun and the planets, eclipses, and the signs of the zodiac. In his villa at Poggio a Cajano, where he introduced a breed of wild ox now common all over Italy, he would immerse himself in the beauties of woods and streams, and in rare plants brought to him from far-off places. Like his mother before him, he composed songs (like "Rispetti," still sung today) and wrote poems (like *La Caccia Con Falcone*—"The Hawking Party"—still read today). If he had no conspicuous ability as a military commander, he compensated for this with the subtlety and shrewdness of his diplomacy—with which he often achieved his objectives without resorting to warfare.

The only attribute that fortune withheld from Lorenzo was that of good looks. Although his frame was impressive in its stature and strength, his features, even in contemporary medallions by Bertoldo and Pollajuolo, both of whom would be careful not to give offense, are hardly attractive. His death mask clearly shows a saddle nose, which—taken in conjunction with his high voice, his lack of any sense of smell, and his early death from what was diagnosed as gout—has suggested to some modern historians that he may have inherited syphilis through his mother. His brother Giuliano was, by contrast, a man of extraordinary beauty and superb health.

The chief crisis of Lorenzo's rule was caused by what is known as the Pazzi Conspiracy of 1478. The Pazzi, being bankers, had long been rivals of the Medici, but it is unlikely that they would have plotted against the lives of Lorenzo and his brother Giuliano had they not been encouraged by Pope Sixtus IV. Sixtus, son of a Ligurian fisherman, had been a Franciscan friar when, on the death of Paul II in 1471, he was raised to the papacy. Like many a common man elevated to the See of Rome, he had immediately thought of what he could do for his humble family. Despite their lack of qualification, spiritual or intellectual, for such elevation, he made two of his nephews cardinals. When one of this pair died prematurely as a result of a life of constant dissipation, Sixtus heaped the dead man's younger brother, Girolamo Riario, with equivalent honors and privileges. Among these was the suzerainty of the town of Imola, east of the Tuscan Appenines. To have a representative of papal power so close to the borders of Florence by no means pleased Lorenzo, and his apprehension was sharpened when he learned that Sixtus had an eye on some other small dominions in the area. Not wishing to risk an open confrontation, Lorenzo began to plot stealthily against Sixtus and his protégé.

The protégé, meanwhile, was himself plotting with the Pazzi clan to murder Lorenzo and his brother. These conspirators soon drew in as an accomplice Francesco Salviati, who bore a grudge against Lorenzo for having prevented him from assuming the post of Archbishop of Pisa, to which Sixtus had elevated him. Not long before, as it happened, Galeazzo Maria Sforza, duke of Milan, had been stabbed to death in church. Murderers being, all too often, men of limited imagination, so lacking in invention that they imitate each other, it was decided to set upon the two Medici brothers while they were attending mass in the Duomo. Francesco de' Pazzi and a certain Bernardo Bandini were to fall upon Giuliano while a well-known papal *condottiere*, Giovanni Battista di Montesecco, was attending to Lorenzo. Montesecco, showing an unaccustomed delicacy, refused this task, however, saying that he could not perform it "in a place where Christ would surely see him." Two priests, Antonio Maffei of Volterra and Stefano da Bagnone, proved to have no such scruples, explaining that "since they were familiar with churches, they would not mind."

So sure were the Medici of their hold on the city that they had no suspicion of what was in store. It is possible that Giuliano was visited by some presentiment though, since he at first absented himself from Mass on the fatal day, on the pretext that he was ill. However, Francesco de' Pazzi and Bandini went to fetch him in simulated friendship, making sure, as they embraced him, that he was not wearing a coat of mail under his jerkin. At some moment in the ser-

vice—tradition has it at the Elevation of the Host—the conspirators fell upon their victims. Giuliano died beneath a rain of dagger blows; his chief assailant, Francesco de' Pazzi, attacking him with such a demented fury that he even wounded himself. Lorenzo was able to fight off his assailants, who were less violent in their attacks, and he and his defenders then fled through the great bronze doors of the Sacristy, dragging with them the body of Francesco di Nori, an intimate who had been slain while going to the defense of Giuliano. Lorenzo had received a slight wound in the throat, and, despite his remonstrances, this was sucked clean by his friend Antonio Ridolfi—in case the dagger that had inflicted it had been poisoned at the tip.

Jacopo de' Pazzi, head of his treacherous family, rode exultantly through the streets, trying to rally the Florentines to his cause with cries of *Popolo e liberta*! But the only answer he got was *Pelle!*—"Balls!"—a reference to the three gold balls on the Medici crest—from an enraged mob that soon began to wreak horrible revenge on the conspirators. Many of them were hanged from the windows of the Palazzo Vecchio, the archbishop in his last throes fixing his teeth in Francesco de' Pazzi as they dangled side by side. The two priests, discovered cowering in the Benedictine abbey in the city, were torn to pieces. Although he had declined to play an active part, Montesecco was beheaded in the courtyard of the Bargello. Only the young Cardinal Riario survived, and he was put under detention.

The conspiracy had failed, yet the Medici were far from out of danger. Furious at the outcome, Sixtus first excommunicated Lorenzo, presumably on the grounds that he had not submitted to his own murder, and then, calling on a long-time papal ally, the King of Naples, to support him, launched a war against Florence. In retaliation Lorenzo assembled an army of mercenaries and called on his own allies, Venice and Milan. Unfortunately, the former city was engaged in a war of its own against the Turks and the latter was rent by internal dissensions—and neither was in a position to assist the beleaguered Lorenzo. As a result, Sixtus IV and King Ferrante of Naples came very close to destroying Florence before the advent of winter put a halt to hostilities.

Lorenzo now decided to make a secret journey from Pisa to Naples in the hope that by confronting Ferrante in person he could detach him from the alliance with Sixtus. It was an extraordinarily brave action in an epoch when what we now regard as virtually sacrosanct rules of diplomatic immunity were as often breached as observed: there was every possibility that the king might imprison or even kill Lorenzo for his pains. However, Lorenzo won over Ferrante with the charm and tact he possessed in such abundance. On payment of a considerable indemnity and the concession of some territory, he was able to return to Florence with a treaty of peace signed not merely by the king but, grudgingly, by Sixtus himself—who nonetheless refused to lift his excommunication of Lorenzo. This last act had to await the occasion when the Turks for the first time succeeded in capturing Italian soil, the Neopolitan harbor of Otranto falling to them in 1480. It was clear that all Italians must unite against this threat

from a people alien in both race and religion, and Sixtus, eager for Lorenzo's help, at last relented.

In gratitude for the defeat of the Pitti Conspiracy in 1466, Sandro Botticelli had already painted his *Adoration of the Magi*—now to be seen in the Uffizi—at the request of Piero de' Medici. In that masterpiece Piero himself kneels, dressed in scarlet, before the Virgin and Child. Lorenzo is on the extreme right, Giuliano on the left. Dead Cosimo, *Pater Patriae*, is at the Child's feet, and there are other Medici and their closest friends ranged around. Now, the Medici having survived an even greater danger, one in which one of their number, Giuliano, had actually been slain, Botticelli painted another commemorative picture. This is his allegorical *Pallas Subduing the Centaur*, lost for many generations and then discovered, rolled up and stored away in the Pitti Palace, by an Englishman, W. Spence, in 1894. The centaur, a symbol of unjust war and so of the Pazzi conspiracy and the hostilities that followed it, shrinks like a frightened dog from the outstretched arm of Pallas, goddess of wisdom, whose dress is covered with Lorenzo's private crest of interlinked diamond rings. Behind her is the bay of Naples, where Lorenzo achieved his diplomatic triumph.

By 1480 Lorenzo was in such a strong position, both within Florence and without, that historian G. F. Young can accurately describe him as having become "the needle of the Italian compass." Having seen what hazards war could bring to Florence, he adopted the role of pacifier at a time when the belligerent Sixtus IV and the heads of most of the other leading city-states were forming and reforming alli-

ances and endlessly making war on each other. With foresight these others lacked, Lorenzo saw it was essential that Italians should preserve peace among themselves. Only a united Italy would be ready to meet the threat posed by the youthful Charles VIII of France, who had succeeded the more prudent Louis XI in 1483 and who now nursed an ambition to recover the lost Angevin throne of Naples, even though he himself was a Valois. The throne had been seized by the Spanish house of Aragon, and rivalry between France and Spain in Italy was to be a constant source of turmoil for years to come.

Ostensibly, Florence was still on the same amicable terms with France as it had been during that period when Piero, virtually adopted into the French royal family, had been granted the privilege of incorporating the French fleur-de-lis into the Medici coat-of-arms. It was vital to Florence that this semblance of amity be preserved, since the Medici Bank, which had suffered bankruptcy in the Netherlands and a decline in profits from a number of other countries, relied on France for much of its business. But it was undoubtedly fear and distrust of France that impelled Lorenzo, after years of conflict with Pope Sixtus IV, to do his utmost to achieve friendly relations with his successor, Innocent VIII. So successful was he in realizing this aim that, within a year of Innocent's accession in 1484, Lorenzo had persuaded the new pope to make his son Giovanni a cardinal at the extraordinarily early age of fourteen.

Three years after this, the always ailing Lorenzo succumbed to an illness from which it was clear, at the onset, he would not recover. Tradition, by no

means infallible, has it that on his deathbed at the Villa Careggi Lorenzo expressed a wish to be shriven by the Dominican monk Savonarola—this despite the fact that Savonarola, who had returned to Florence one year before after a long absence in Lombardy, had filled his fiery sermons, which drew huge crowds to San Marco, with denunciations of the profligacy, corruption, and godlessness of the Medici family. According to this account—increasingly thought to have been fabricated by the ambitious Dominicans when Lorenzo was no longer alive to deny it—the humble monk declined to give absolution to the magnificent ruler until he had fulfilled three conditions: first, Lorenzo was to repent his sins; second, he was to return all public property he had wrongfully appropriated; and third, he was to restore to Florence the liberty his family had taken from it. Lorenzo assented to the first two of these conditions, but when the third was put to him he turned his face to the wall. At that Savonarola is said to have departed, having refused his blessing. According to Angelo Poliziano, one of Lorenzo's closest friends, however, nothing of this kind happened: the dying Lorenzo asked for absolution—and Savonarola promptly granted it.

The sixteenth-century historian Francesco Guicciardini wrote that Lorenzo's death was "bitter for him, since he was not quite forty-four years of age, and bitter for his republic, which because of his prudence, reputation and intelligence in everything honorable and excellent, flourished marvelously with riches and all those ornaments and advantages with which a long peace is usually accompanied."

*"States cannot be ruled by prayers," the pragmatic
Cosimo de Medici was fond of observing; but by 1481
Cosimo was dead and a zealous monk by the name of
Girolamo Savonarola had come to San Marco. From
that pulpit he disputed Cosimo's practical dictum and
defied his heirs. States not only could but should be
ruled by prayers, he insisted, and his increasingly bitter
jeremiads so stirred the populace of Florence that they
eventually drove Cosimo's great-grandson Piero into
exile. Four years later, in 1498, the tables turned. After
a night of resistance in a local monastery, the renegade
monk was compelled to give himself up to his enemies:
the fires lit by Savonarola to burn the books and
paintings he thought profane were now waiting for him.
The portrait opposite is one of two that Fra
Bartolommeo executed of Savonarola after his death.*

There is justice in this appraisal of a man who, in addition to preserving Florence from outside destruction by his diplomacy and courage, cast over it the constant illumination of his singular presence. His was a period in which everything seemed possible: one day four lost books of Cicero would turn up; another day a giraffe would arrive from the sultan of Egypt (and be immortalized in paintings by Andrea del Sarto, Franciabiagio, and Piero di Cosimo). If Ficino bore the title of *Pater Platonicae familiae,* father of the Platonic Academy, then Lorenzo was its generous uncle. He was a poet of outstanding talent, with a rare appreciation of the beauty of the Tuscan landscape and a rarer understanding of the people.

Unfortunately, Lorenzo's son and heir, Piero, had none of these qualities—and two years after his father's death he had to cope with a situation as difficult as any faced by Lorenzo. In 1494, determined to annex the Kingdom of Naples, Charles VIII crossed the Alps into Italy and, since Piero was an ally of King Ferrante, made at once for Florence. In one of the most humiliating moments in Medici history, Piero was obliged to go out to the French encampment and plead with Charles to spare the city. This the king contemptuously agreed to do—on the condition that Pisa be ceded to him. Furious at what they regarded as a craven betrayal, the Florentines drove Piero and his family out of the city, themselves entered into negotiations with Charles, and then set up the most democratic government Florence had enjoyed since 1382. A Great Council of some three thousand members was prorogued as a legislative body and, in order to house it, the huge

Salone dei Cinquecento was constructed in the Palazzo Vecchio, with Simone dei Pollaiuolo, known as Cronaca, as architect. A few years later, in 1503, Michelangelo and Leonardo da Vinci were commissioned by *gonfalonier* Piero Soderini to produce frescoes to decorate the walls. Michelangelo, dealing with the 1440 battle of Anghiari against Milan, sketched a cartoon, or preliminary study, of a group of soldiers bathing in the Arno, depicting them at the very moment a trumpet summons them to arms. He proceeded no further, however. Leonardo, dealing with the 1364 battle of Cascina against a Pisan army, drew the famous scene known as the Battle of the Standard—and he actually began painting on the walls. These cartoons played the same part in the art of the fifteenth century as Masaccio's frescoes in the Carmine had played in the fourteenth. Between them, two supremely gifted artists had briefly turned the palazzo into *la scuola del mondo,* the school of the world in art, with the young Raphael as one of their most ardent pupils. Unfortunately, though Vasari gives a full description of each cartoon, neither survives; copies of portions of each by lesser artists suggest how much we have lost.

The man largely responsible for bringing about this re-emergence of republicanism and for guiding it according to his theocratic vision was the Dominican monk Girolamo Savonarola. A native of Ferrara, he had, in his early youth, written a treatise entitled "On a Disregard of the World" and was already in the habit of offering up the prayer "O Lord, make known to me the way in which I must guide my soul." He then spent several years living the life of

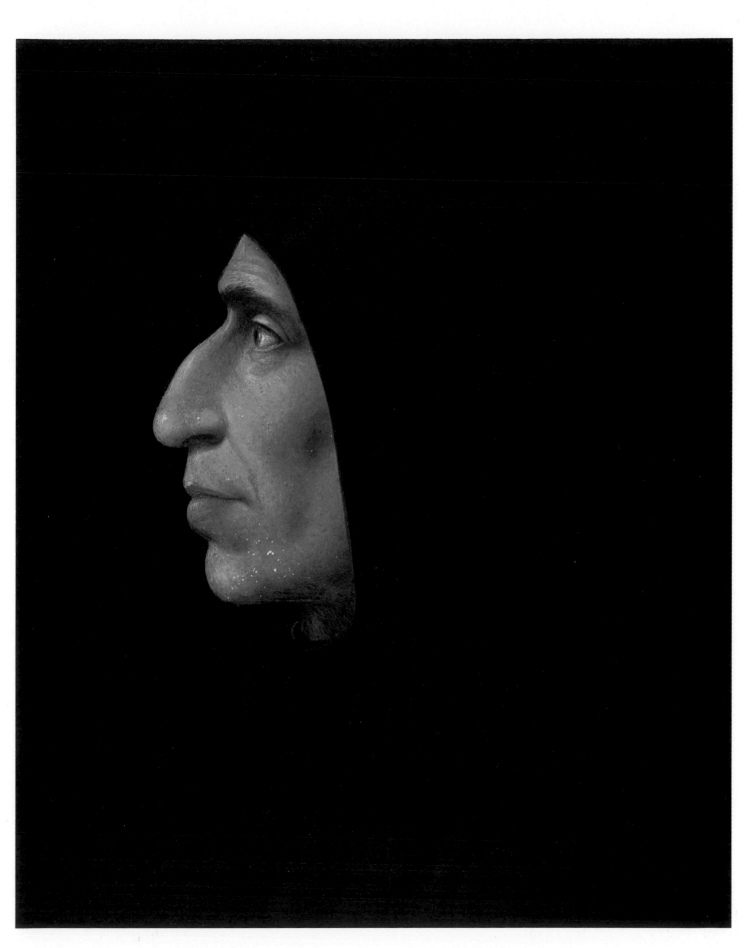

an ascetic in a monastery in Bologna, where he slept on a bed of twigs, fasted continuously, and devoted himself to the writings of St. Augustine, Cassian, and the Bible. In 1482 he moved to Florence, but because his sermons failed to attract the worldly and sophisticated Florentines—a surprise in view of his subsequent fame as a preacher—his stay was brief.

That Savonarola returned seven years later to Florence was largely due to the influence of Pico della Mirandola, an intimate of Lorenzo and a member of the Platonic Academy. Hearing Savonarola preach in Reggio, Pico was so impressed that he begged Lorenzo to elevate this obscure monk from his humble cloister in Lombardy to the glory of the priorate of San Marco—which Lorenzo did with what proved to be fatal results for the Medici.

So great were Savonarola's audiences that he was obliged to preach in the garden of San Marco instead of the church. Then, during Lent in 1491, his audiences having grown larger still, he moved on to preach in the Duomo. It was there, for a period of eight years, that this Renaissance ayatollah would thrill his impressionable audiences with fulminations against luxury, covetousness, usury, fornication, and sodomy. He also recommended that the Signoria use torture on gamblers and urged servants to spy on their masters. His pulpit had become a throne, and members of the noble houses had become his adherents. Peasants flocked to Florence from the surrounding countryside to hang on his every word. Rich women abandoned their jewels for him—and some even abandoned their husbands and took the veil.

At the height of Savonarola's power a huge bonfire was built in the Signoria and his followers, who called themselves *piagnoni*, or weepers, hurled onto it extravagant gowns, priceless jewelry, false hair, masks, scents, and studies from the nude (many of them by Fra Bartolommeo). Merely because they were beautiful, an illuminated codex of Petrarch and several codices of Boccaccio were consigned to the flames by crowds that leapt and danced to the exultant hymns of Girolamo Benivieni. Overwhelmed by all this revivalist fervor, Botticelli decided to give up painting because it was the work of the Devil.

Florence, Savonarola repeatedly declared, was corrupt; and in that he was right, since all humanity is, to some extent, corrupt. What he failed to appreciate was that out of this corruption there had come—and there would continue to come—a greatness and beauty unparalleled since Greek and Roman times. Over the gate of the Palazzo Vecchio were written the words "Jesus Christ is the King of Florence," and although he never accepted any office in the Signoria, Savonarola clearly regarded himself as prime minister to that king. His functionaries now included the *lustratori* (purifiers), the *limosinieri* (collectors of alms), and the *moralisti*, whose task it was to clear houses of playing cards, musical instruments, and books that were not concerned with Christian devotion.

Savonarola sealed his own doom when his attacks extended from the powerful of Florence to the Borgia pope Alexander VI, who had refused to give up his support of the French monarch Charles VIII. This previously obscure little monk fulminated,

A gallery of quattrocento Florentine portraits, from the hands of that city's most talented fifteenth-century artists. From left to right: Botticelli's three-quarter profile of Giuliano de Medici; Ghirlandaio's study of the pensive Lucrezia Sommaria; a portrait of an anonymous Florentine youth by Filippino Lippi; another youth, younger but likewise unknown, attributed to Biagio d'Antonio; and, at near left, Leonardo da Vinci's amply fleshed young woman.

"Prepare thyself, O Rome, for great shalt be thy punishment, thou shalt be hemmed in with iron, and given up to the sword, the fire and the flame!" It is hardly surprising, under the circumstances, that Alexander VI should have finally decided that enough was enough. Sure that a measure so drastic would bring Savonarola to heel, he pronounced his excommunication—but Savonarola went on preaching, remarking merely that "When the Pope orders what is wrong, he does not order it as Pope."

Always fickle, the Florentines began now to turn against the renegade priest in increasing numbers. They shouted abuse at him when he preached, and they accused his *piagnoni* of hypocrisy and attacked them physically. Savonarola thereupon withdrew to San Marco. As a test of his saintliness, an ordeal by fire was arranged in the Loggia de' Lanzi, with one of Savonarola's most faithful Dominican disciples, Fra Domenico da Pescia, competing against a friar of the rival Franciscan order. On the appointed day, huge crowds collected as though for a circus, a passage was made through a rectangular pile of firewood, and the two champions—each with his singing and praying entourage—awaited the application of the brand that would set the firewood alight. Nothing comparable had taken place for almost half a century; it was as though the Renaissance, with its sweeping away of superstition, had never taken place. The Signoria, hostile to Savonarola, had no real intention of giving the mob the spectacle it desired, and one objection after another was raised by the Franciscans and was considered at length by the Signoria. Then rain began to fall, soaking judges, participants, and spectators with an impartiality previously lacking in the proceedings, and the Signoria declared that the contest must be abandoned. For this loss of a long-awaited entertainment, the public unjustly blamed Savonarola.

Eventually, Savonarola was seized from his monastery, taken to the Palazzo Vecchio, and placed in a tiny cell in the same tower where Cosimo had been incarcerated many years earlier. Under constant torture he apparently confessed to the offenses of claiming to have supernatural powers and of fomenting rebellion. He was condemned to execution, and on May 23, 1498, in the Piazza della Signoria, he and two of his closest companions were first hanged and then burned before a huge crowd. As his friar's gown was stripped from him, Savonarola said: "Sacred gown, thou wert granted to me by the grace of God and I have kept thee unblemished. Now I forsake thee not but thou are taken from me." The bishop rebuked him: "I separate thee from the Church militant and triumphant." To which Savonarola retorted calmly: "Militant, yes, but not triumphant, since that does not rest with you."

Thanks to Fra Bartolommeo della Porta, so fervent an admirer of Savonarola that for four years after his death he never took up a brush, we have two haunting portraits of this ascetic visionary, one of which can be seen in his cell, No. 12, in San Marco. The inscription, *Hieronymi Ferrariensis a Deo missi prophetae effigies*—"the Image of Girolamo of Ferrara, prophet sent by God"—was concealed at the time of Savonarola's trial for fear that a claim so extravagant might further alienate his judges.

The most famous of the many gardens in Florence are the largest—the Boboli. Laid out in 1549 by Tribolo and augmented later in that same century by both Ammannati and Buontalenti, they form an enormous, verdant irregular polyhedron between the Pitti Palace and Fort Belvedere on the south bank of the Arno. The Boboli Grotto, which Buontalenti designed, lies at the southern end of the gardens, as does the open-air theatre seen at near left. Less famous—and therefore less frequented—are the city's numerous smaller parks and private gardens. Of these, few are more carefully tended or lushly lovely than those surrounding Sir Harold Acton's villa (below).

VI

The Long Day Wanes

In the interregnum between the death of Savonarola in 1498 and the return of the Medici in 1512, Florence, like the rest of Italy, was constantly threatened by anarchy within and domination from without. After three years of chaos following Savonarola's martyrdom, the Florentines attempted to solve their internal problems by appointing a *gonfalonier*, Piero Soderini, for life; but despite his good intentions Soderini had little capacity for government, leading sixteenth-century historian Francesco Guicciardini to this damning conclusion: "It is difficult to imagine a city so thoroughly shattered and ill-regulated as ours was at this time."

The Florentines tried to end the constant threat of invasion by siding with their old ally, France, against the combined forces of the papacy, Naples, Venice, and—a new factor in the power struggle—Spain. Unfortunately, Louis XII's campaigns in Italy ended in disaster, and Florence, bereft of this source of protection, made the prudent decision to seek an accommodation with Julius II, a pope so warlike that he took pleasure in leading his own armies into battle. The price of this reversal of policy was, first, a large indemnity—which Florence, once so wealthy, could ill afford in 1512—and second, the return of the Medici to the city. Henceforth the government of the city would be directed by puppets of Lorenzo's second son, Giovanni, who, in February 1513, succeeded Julius II as Pope Leo X.

Paradoxically, it was precisely at this time, when the political fortunes of Florence were so abject, that its achievements in the arts reached their apogee. In the year 1505, when the survival of Florence as an independent state seemed in grave doubt, six of the greatest painters that the world has ever known—Leonardo da Vinci, Raphael, Fra Bartolommeo, Lorenzo di Credi, Michelangelo, and Perugino—were all working in the city. Unhappily, in the years that followed Rome and other powerful city-states would make claims on most of these artists, claims Florence found itself in no position to resist.

Piero de' Medici having died in exile in 1505, the representative of Leo X in Florence was his brother Giuliano, Duke of Nemours. He was assisted by a cousin, Giulio, the natural son of that Giuliano de' Medici who had been murdered in the Pazzi Conspiracy. Leo X died in 1516 and was succeeded as ruler of Florence by his nephew Lorenzo, son of the late Piero and father of a lone child, Catherine de' Medici, who, as the wife of Henri II of France, was to become as famous as any of her family. When Lorenzo died in 1519 at the age of twenty-seven, the succession should have passed to descendants of old Giovanni's second son, but Giulio had other plans. Illegitimate himself, he had fathered an illegitimate son, Alessandro, for whom he coveted control of Florence. To achieve this end Giulio first moved into the Medici Palace himself and then, when he was obliged to return to Rome in order to fulfill his duties as cardinal—and, eventually, as pope—he made Cardinal Passerini his deputy, charged with safeguarding the interests of his heir. Gathered together under the roof of the Medici Palace were a number of discordant elements: Cardinal Passerini, watchful of the interests of the man who was shortly to become Pope Clement VII; the dead Lorenzo's

daughter, Catherine de' Medici, who was soon to be removed to a convent; the dead Giuliano's illegitimate son, Ippolito; and Alessandro, illegitimate son of the pope-to-be.

Clement VII's scheming on behalf of his illegitimate son was temporarily checked in 1527 when the new pope, having made an ill-advised alliance with a former papal enemy, Francis I of France, had to look on impotently from the Castel S. Angelo while the forces of the emperor, Charles V, descended on Rome and put the city to sack. As soon as the news of this disaster reached the republicans in Florence, they sent the Medici clan packing once again.

These republicans soon made a miscalculation as grievous as Clement's, however. After three years, during which the Medici languished in exile in Orvieto and the upright Niccolo Capponi ruled Florence as *gonfalonier*, Clement VII patched up his quarrel with the emperor. He did this by crowning Charles V in Rome and by marrying off his illegitimate son, Alessandro, to the emperor's daughter, Margherita. He then set about regaining Florence for his family. This task was facilitated by the treachery of a mercenary commander, Malatesta Baglioni, who defected from the Florentines to Clement's side. After a ten-month siege during which Michelangelo designed new defenses for the city, the Florentines, weakened by hunger and disease, were obliged to surrender.

In 1531 Alessandro arrived with great pomp in Florence, and the following year, the Republic having been declared at an end, he became duke. Called "The Moor" because of his dark complexion, Alessandro made his first act one of vandalism: the great bell of the Palazzo Vecchio, which had so often called the citizens of Florence to defend their independence and which, having a great deal of silver in its compound, weighed eleven tons, was hurled from its campanile and smashed into fragments.

The true Medici heir, Ippolito, a studious and gentle man, deemed it inadvisable to remain in Florence in close propinquity to his cousin Alessandro and took himself off to Bologna, where he found the writing of poetry an occupation more congenial than political intrigue. However, after the death of Clement VII in 1535, the Florentines, sickened by the cruel and autocratic rule of Alessandro, approached this mild exile and requested that he head a mission to Charles V, asking the emperor to intercede on their behalf. Hearing what was afoot, Alessandro promptly hired an assassin to kill Ippolito. Alessandro himself was stabbed to death by a cousin, Lorenzino de' Medici, only a year later—further proof of the adage that those who live by the sword die by it. Lorenzino, a Renaissance Brutus, was to be the hero of a tragedy, *Lorenzoaccio*, by the nineteenth-century French poet Alfred de Musset.

The rule of Florence now passed to Cosimo I, son of Giovanni delle Bande Nere, probably the greatest *condottiere* of the time. Giovanni, descended not from Cosimo Pater Patriae but from Cosimo's younger brother, Lorenzo, had died at the age of twenty-eight, after a life of frenetic adventure, leaving behind a wife and a single child, Cosimo. This youth, who was only eighteen in 1537, had himself declared Alessandro's successor through a combina-

tion of his own quiet self-assurance in advancing his claims and the influence of a distant cousin, Cardinal Cibò. Charles V himself confirmed the choice of Cosimo, who promptly proved that the emperor's confidence was not misplaced by decisively defeating those Florentines who had rebelled against his accession in a battle at Montemurlo, a few miles from Florence, in 1537. Shrewdly sensing that Alessandro's murderer, Lorenzino, might be thought to have a stronger claim than his own, Cosimo outlawed him and put a price on his head. (Lorenzino survived for eleven years in his place of exile, Venice, before two professional killers at last succeeded in tracking him down, catching him unawares, and stabbing him to death.)

In 1539 Cosimo married Eleanora of Toledo, daughter of Don Pedro, Viceroy of Naples. She is familiar to us in the stiff brocades and milky pearls of the Bronzino portrait in the Uffizi, from which she looks out with an expression of settled melancholy—as though she had a premonition of the terrible tragedy that was to occur in 1552, when, within days of each other, she and two of her sons were to die of a particularly virulent form of malaria. Enemies of the Medici, always eager to blacken their name, spread the calumny that one of the boys had killed the other in the course of a quarrel; that Cosimo, beside himself with grief, had then killed the culprit; and that Eleanora had died from the shock of witnessing these events. They could produce no evidence for this improbable scenario, however, and all but the most gullible Florentines eventually came to accept the truth concerning this triple tragedy.

Cosimo had inherited from his ancestors a strong mercantile instinct—a boon, because in the unsettled period since the death of Lorenzo the Magnificent, the business of the Medici had suffered a sharp decline. Cosimo now set about reviving the Medici's financial empire, recognizing that money was of prime importance in realizing his ambitions both for his dynasty and the state. He intensified commercial relations with England and Spain, Antwerp and Augsburg; and because there was now brisk competition from Flanders, France, and England in the woollen industry, once dominated by Florence, he wisely began to extend the Medici interests in mining. (This was all the more important because France, previously a lavish buyer of Florentine silk, had begun to create a silk industry of its own.) In addition, Cosimo was instrumental in introducing new crafts to his domain: he brought artisans from Sicily to Pisa to give instruction in the working of coral, and from Murano to Florence to give instruction in the manufacture of glass. He even lured a young Frenchman from Rome in 1568 to instruct local craftsmen in what was to become a specialty of Florence—the art of *pietra dura*, or mosaic.

Cosimo was no less assiduous in shoring up the political, as distinct from the commercial, underpinnings of his autocratic rule. When Machiavelli wrote *The Prince* in 1527, he had just such a ruler in mind. His prince ruthlessly eliminates all those who pose a threat to his authority, breaks promises if it is to his advantage to do so, tells lies in self-justification or self-aggrandisement, sets one ally or counselor against another, and schemes against even those

"The old treasure bridge," Ruskin calls it in Mornings in Florence, *adding that the Ponte Vecchio is the "most precious historical link of all, tottering under the weight of shops and galleries." The first of those shops were run by butchers, but over the years they gave way to goldsmiths' shops. It is especially appropriate, then, that a bust of Cellini, master jeweler of the Renaissance, should stand today in the little piazza at the center of the bridge, not far from the spot where that greatest of novelists, Charles Dickens, stood to make his famed observation: "The space of one house, in the centre, being left open, the view beyond is shown as in a frame; and that precious glimpse of sky, and water, and rich buildings, shining so quietly among the huddled roofs and gables on the bridge, is exquisite." The huddled roofs and gables are still there, as is the space of one house left open in the center, but the Ponte Vecchio does indeed totter today, burdened as it is with the upper gallery that Cosimo added to connect the Palazzo Vecchio with his newly finished Pitti Palace.*

who seem to be dearest to him. Whether, in presenting such a character, Machiavelli—once a devoted servant of the Republic—was writing admiringly or ironically, has long been the subject of debate. The spirit of the Renaissance had been to reject the narrow Christian values of the time in favor of those of classical Greek and Rome. Machiavelli's prince was to reject even the Ciceronian virtues of magnanimity, honesty, and tolerance.

Taciturn and aloof, Cosimo gathered around him men who were not so much advisers in shaping his policies as minions to carry them out. By abolishing all distinction between guildsmen and non-guildsmen and between major and minor guilds, he made it cruelly clear that all his subjects were equal in their subservience to him. Moreover, Cosimo's domain was not Florence alone but the whole of Tuscany—and it was therefore a fundamental aim of his policy to acquire the still-independent city-state of Siena. His opportunity came when France and Spain, perpetually in conflict, began yet another war in 1555. Rightly sensing that Spain would be the victor, Cosimo sided with Charles V—and when imperial forces stormed Siena and captured it, he received the city as his reward.

By this annexation, and others less important, Cosimo almost doubled the size of his original domains; and though, with the discovery of the Americas and increasing trade with the Far East, Florence was no longer as important a power in Europe, Cosimo ensured that it remained an important power in Italy. A brilliant administrator, he was able to give his subjects the kind of orderly government

they had wholly lacked during the previous half-century of turbulence and constant change. The price, as of every absolutist regime, was that their independence was forfeited—and it is to this loss of independence that some historians attribute the decline in Florentine culture during the next two centuries.

In the year 1569 Pius V published a papal bull creating Cosimo Grand Duke of Tuscany (although, in fact, this prerogative lay with the emperor, at that time fully occupied with a war in Germany). In the following year the pope crowned Cosimo in Rome, and gradually all Europe, including Spain and Germany, came to recognize the elevation. In achieving his crown, Cosimo had demonstrated true Machiavellian ruthlessness. Even when Cosimo had been elevated to the papacy, Pius V had still continued to persecute heretics with the same zeal he had shown as Inquisitor, and one of those he pursued with particular venom was Cosimo's friend and counselor, Pietro Carnesecchi. After a career in the Roman church that had gained him the rank of Protonotary to Clement VII, Carnesecchi had been converted to Protestantism. On becoming pope, Pius V had demanded that Cosimo yield up this heretic, and Cosimo, no doubt mindful of the crown on which his heart was set, complied—as Machiavelli's prince would certainly have done in similar circumstances. Carnesecchi was tortured and then burned by the Inquisition in Rome in October 1567; and with the extinction of his life, the reforming spirit, previously strong in Italy, was also extinguished.

Cosimo was a generous patron of the arts even though he lacked the instinctive taste of Lorenzo the

Magnificent. He often supported second-rate artists and withheld patronage from first-rate ones. Thus Baccio Bandinelli received many commissions—of which he seldom showed himself worthy—while the talented Niccolò Pericolo Tribolo, for lack of encouragement, degenerated into a decorator of gardens and fountains and arranger of such state occasions as the bridal entry of Eleanora of Toledo into Florence and the baptism of Eleanora and Cosimo's eldest son, Francesco, in the Baptistery. Giorgio Vasari always exerted a strong influence on Cosimo, but he was more distinguished as a man of art than as an original artist.

But if Cosimo often lacked natural discernment for the new, he was full of inherited enthusiasm for the old. When the Medici were expelled from Florence in 1497 and 1527, their collections were dispersed, with some items going abroad and others to rival families. Cosimo had these sought out, and, with advice from Vasari and Bronzino, he began to assemble them in a new palace—one now known as the Pitti Palace but known, during Medici rule, as the Grand Ducal Palace or the Royal Palace—on the other side of the Arno. (The Palazzo Vecchio had grown too cramped for himself, his long-suffering wife, and their nine children.) Vasari tells us that Brunelleschi was the architect of the original edifice, built for Luca Pitti, whose descendants, short of money, sold it to Cosimo's wife; but it is now thought more probable that the palace was the work of Luca Fancelli. It was to Bartolommeo Ammannati that Cosimo entrusted the task of refurbishing, extending, and embellishing the original structure in a

manner worthy of his status. The result is an edifice that, though some critics have found it too squat and rough, fully deserves both George Eliot's praise—"A wonderful union of cyclopean massiveness with stately regularity"—and Taine's—"I doubt if there is a more monumental palace in the whole of Europe; I have never seen one that left me with a comparable impression of grandeur and simplicity." Cosimo, who was the founder of the oldest botanical gardens in Europe, those at Pisa, and of the Giardino Botannico dei Semplici in Florence, took a personal interest in the laying out, first under Tribolo and later under Bernardo Buontalenti and Giulio and Alfonso Parigi, of the Boboli Gardens, set on the slope behind his new residence.

To join the Palazzo Vecchio—which had been considerably enlarged and ornamented when he moved to it from the Palazzo Medici in 1540—with his new Pitti Palace, Cosimo had a passage constructed across the Arno by way of the Ponte Vecchio. The effect of this addition to the graceful bridge was unfortunate, imposing a straight line on a construction that would look far better without one and obstructing the view through its previously open loggia. It was while this passage—suggested by Homer's description of the passage uniting the palaces of Hector and Priam—was being built that Cosimo encountered Camilla Martelli, daughter of one of the jewelers on the bridge, who became first his mistress and then, after the death of Eleanora, his wife—much to the disgust of his sons, who refused publicly to recognize as their father's lawful wife and their stepmother someone so low born.

111

Another palace built by Cosimo was the Uffizi. "Who were the Uffizi?" is a question sometimes asked by foreign visitors who do not appreciate that in Italian *uffizi* merely means "offices." The building was so called because, at the time of its erection in 1560, it was used to house the municipal offices previously accommodated in the Palazzo Vecchio, which had been appropriated by Cosimo as a Medici residence.

It was Cosimo who, in 1557, resolved to rebuild a more glorious Ponte Santa Trinita after floods swept away the original structure, and he asked Vasari to draw up the plans in consultation with Michelangelo, then at work in Rome. These plans were given to Bartolommeo Ammannati, who executed them between 1567 and 1569 at a cost of 46,000 scudi. (This cost was borne not, as might have been expected, by Cosimo but by the people of Florence.) Cosimo also commissioned Giovanni Battista del Tasso to build the Mercato Nuovo, with its exquisitely proportioned columns and its arched roof. It opened in 1547 as a market for silk and gold; its chief modern commodity is objects made of straw. Florentines refer to it as the Porcellino, or Piglet, because of a famous bronze boar, copied by Pietro Tacca from a Roman marble now in the Uffizi, that stands in it. Lovers of Hans Christian Andersen will remember that it was while riding this creature that his little urchin enjoyed so many adventures.

Cosimo showed an intense interest in the Etruscan past of his domains, financing excavations at the site of ancient Clusium, home of Lars Porsena, at Arezzo, and at other settlements in the region. His descendants continued this search, with the result that the Archaeological Museum of Florence now contains what is probably the finest collection of Etruscan remains in existence. Cosimo also laid the foundations of the collection of Egyptian antiquities displayed in the same museum.

On the old principle of giving a subject people circuses as well as bread, this most astute of rulers introduced to Florence chariot races of the kind that used to be held in ancient Rome. The site of this entertainment was the Piazza Santa Maria Novella, where it is still possible to see the goalposts of Serravezza marble, supported on bronze tortoises created by Giambologna, that were erected to replace the original wooden ones. Cosimo also repaired and completed the Laurentian Library, already housed in the magnificent building that Michelangelo had designed for Pope Clement VII. He had many of the manuscripts rebound, bought the valuable collection of Cardinal Carpi, and added works from abbeys and convents throughout Tuscany.

Cosimo died in 1574, having, through four years of increasing ill-health, left the government of Tuscany to his far from capable son and heir, Francesco. He was buried in San Lorenzo under a tombstone inscribed *Magnus Dux Etruriae Primus*—"First Grand Duke of Etruria." In his ruthlessness, stinginess, and coldness of heart he was a much less attractive character than Cosimo Pater Patriae or Lorenzo the Magnificent, but he certainly achieved a great deal for his people.

After the death of Cosimo the fortunes of the Medici family and those of Florence, things almost syn-

onymous, entered a period of continuous decline. Francesco I, who succeeded his father at the age of thirty-three, inherited many of his father's intellectual gifts but little of his will to rule. The man whom Veronese depicted in a famous portrait as a figure of imposing authority in fact preferred dabbling in science to administering his realm. As a result, inefficiency and corruption soon became rife, and the hatred that these aroused in high and low alike was intensified by an increase in taxes and by a capricious cruelty directed toward anyone deemed likely to thwart Francesco or to whom he took a dislike.

Each time one of the Medici came to power, a plot was sure to be hatched against him by the family's rivals. In this case it was the Pucci, Ridolfi, Capponi, and Machiavelli families who together planned an assassination. Francesco learned of what was happening and at once ordered the ringleaders executed and their property sequestrated. A few managed to make their escape, and they fomented trouble for him from their places of exile.

Francesco's first marriage had been a loveless, dynastic one to the Archduchess Joanna of Austria. Cosimo had arranged the marriage because he wished to ingratiate himself with Joanna's brother, the Emperor Maximilian, in order to obtain the emperor's consent to his being named Archduke of Tuscany by the pope. Francesco was already attached to Bianca Cappello, whom most historians describe as beautiful, though the portraits of her hardly confirm this. Joanna became homesick; Francesco, absorbed with Bianca, no doubt neglected her. In order that she should not complain to the

emperor, Cosimo did everything in his power to make Joanna happy. After his move to the Pitti Palace, he handed over the Palazzo Vecchio to the couple and had its cortile painted with frescoes depicting Austrian towns. Francesco was less inclined to consider his wife's feelings, and after he succeeded Cosimo in 1574 he had a secret underground passage constructed from Bianca Cappello's house, No. 26 Via Maggio, to the Pitti Palace, where he had taken up his residence.

The year after Joanna's death in 1578 Francesco married Bianca. By then much of his time was spent in his laboratory, where he experimented with the melting of rock crystal and the making of vases from it. But like his ancestors Francesco remained a generous patron of arts and literature. Giambologna received a number of commissions from him, most notably for his *Mercury* in the Bargello, the *Rape of the Sabines* in the Loggia dei Lanzi, and the *Dovizia*, or *Abundance*, at the summit of the Boboli Gardens. Tradition has it that this last figure is an idealized representation of Francesco's wife Joanna. It was under the patronage of Francesco that, in 1582, Francesco Garazzini and Leonardo Salviati founded their society, still in existence, for the purification of the Italian language, known as the Accademia della Crusca. *Crusca* means "chaff" in English, and the object of the society was, figuratively, to separate the wheat from the chaff of linguistic usage. More importantly, it was under Francesco that the Uffizi first began to fulfill its present function as an art gallery. Above the second floor, where Cosimo had accommodated a variety of craftsmen, there was an open loggia, which Francesco had Bernardo Buontalenti enclose with glass. Sculptor as well as architect, Buontalenti also executed the statue of his patron, looking somewhat absurd in Roman costume, that stands over the portico at the southern end of the gallery.

It was this same Buontalenti who was at the center of what diarist Francesco Settimani described at the time as "a work of shame, for which, if all the world were to unite in reproving, it could not express blame enough." This came about as the result of a 1586 decision by Senator Buonaccorso Uguccioni that Giotto's façade of the Duomo, with its statues by artists like Donatello and Andrea Pisano, its canopies and columns of porphyry, should be demolished so that a new façade could be erected in its place. Some original statues were saved but many were lost, and the porphyry columns were smashed to pieces. Buontalenti was one of a trio of architects who were each commissioned to prepare an up-to-date design for a new façade. Buontalenti's architectural elevation, with its square doors with architraves, its bare round windows and flat pilasters, was hardly promising—but neither were the other designs, and none was chosen. Indeed, it was not until 1871–87 that a neo-Gothic front designed by Emilio de Farbus was erected.

Francesco was also an astute businessman in the Medici mold. He considerably enlarged his family's fortune by trading not merely within the confines of Italy but throughout the whole of Europe, with the result that, at his death in 1587, he had amassed a hoard of coins, gold, jewelry, and promissory notes.

Francesco and Bianca Cappello died on the same day at the Medici villa of Poggio a Caiano. Because of this coincidence, stories circulated suggesting that either sorcery—Bianca had long been thought by many to be a witch—or poison was involved. The most persistent of these stories held that the couple had plotted to kill Francesco's estranged brother and subsequent heir, Ferdinando, who was then visiting them from Rome. Owing either to an error or to an adroit transposition carried out by their prospective victim or one of his entourage, they had both mistakenly eaten of a poisoned pie intended for him. According to another version, it was Ferdinando who had planned the murder of his brother and sister-in-law, neither of whom he liked.

Historians give little credence to such gossip, however, noting that it was always in the interest of enemies of the Medici to keep such stories in circulation. Bianca had suffered from dropsy for some time, and she had not even been present during the banquet at which Francesco fell ill. In any case, in a period when refrigeration did not exist and the only known preservatives were salt and smoke, food poisoning was not uncommon—even if deaths from it tended to be ascribed to causes more sinister. (Salmonella, we may be sure, was responsible for many more sudden fatalities during the Renaissance than all the Borgias put together.) Nonetheless, Ferdinando seemed to confirm the rumor of his responsibility for the two deaths by replying to Buontalenti's query as to where the Grand Duchess should be buried with the contemptuous "Where you wish. We do not want her among *us.*"

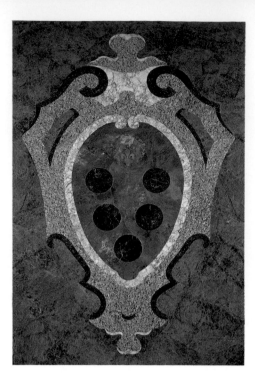

It was Ferdinando, fourth son of Cosimo, who had, at his father's petition, been made cardinal at the astonishingly early age of fourteen. He was thirty-eight when his brother Francesco died, and during his long sojourn in Rome he had achieved a reputation as a stubborn and fearless opponent of any pope with whom he disagreed and as an extravagant and discriminating collector of Greek and Roman art. In the first of these capacities he had often been at loggerheads with the formidable Sixtus V; in the second, he had acquired for his Villa Medici in Rome such classical works as the *Dancing Faun*, the *Venus dei Medici*, and the *Apollino*.

Ferdinando had a boundless respect for his father, Cosimo I, in whose memory he commissioned Giambologna's equestrian statue in the Piazza della Signoria. Like his father, he was a just, if stern, ruler, stamping out the corruption that had become increasingly common during his brother's reign, reorganizing the adminstration of the duchy, and carrying out such public works as the draining of the marshy Val di Chiana and the linking of Pisa and Livorno by means of the Navigilio Canal. It was he who, to all intents and purposes, was the creator of Livorno, described by Montesquieu as "the masterpiece of the dynasty of the Medici," and he who elevated it from a fishing village to a powerful commercial port.

But in Florence itself Ferdinando is now chiefly remembered for his inauguration of the Cappella dei Principi, a mausoleum dedicated to the glory of his family. This gigantic jewel box, on which millions of lire were spent from century to century

The New Sacristy at San Lorenzo (left, below) is the gift of a surpassingly talented sculptor and architect, Michelangelo, to surpassingly dedicated patrons of the arts, the Medici. The sculptor's great statues, Day and Night *(visible at left center in this photograph) and* Dawn and Twilight *preside over the sacristy's austere interior like inhabitants of limbo, frozen in an eternity of grief. Of them Ruskin wrote: "Four ineffable types, not of darkness nor of day—nor of morning nor evening, but of the departure and the resurrection, the twilight and dawn, of the souls of men." By contrast, the Cappella dei Principi or Chapel of the Princes, as the other Medici tomb at San Lorenzo is known, has no such power to touch the soul, having had no animating genius of Michelangelo's stature. It is, instead, a triumph of* pietra dura, *the stone-setter's art—as the intricate pavement detail at far left suggests.*

while the façade of San Lorenzo, the church that encloses it, awaited completion, is cunningly put together from an extravagant variety of stones: jasper, alabaster, lapis lazuli, verde antico, rose agate, marble, mother-of-pearl, coral. Here are sepulchral monuments not merely of Ferdinando's father, Cosimo, and brother, Francesco, but of Ferdinando's son, grandson, and great-grandson—Cosimo II, Ferdinand II, and Cosimo III, respectively.

Inevitably, visitors to San Lorenzo compare this floridly ostentatious edifice with the austerely simple Medici Chapel of an earlier date, built by Michelangelo for Clement VII though he left its decor uncompleted when he quit Florence for Rome in 1534, never to return. Commemorated here are Clement VII's father, Giuliano; his uncle, Lorenzo; and two of his cousins, Giuliano, duke of Nemours, and Lorenzo, duke of Urbino.

The ornamentation of the Chapel of the Princes demanded extreme skill in the art of mosaic. Fortunately, Ferdinando had already founded his Royal Factory of the Pietra Dura, to which the job of decorating the chapel was entrusted. Such elaborate inlay work still is made in Florence, although it is now usually applied to objects far daintier in scale than the Medici mausoleum.

To the encouragement of Ferdinando is also ascribed the emergence of opera. Previously, music had merely provided interludes in the course of a work of drama; but the musicians and music lovers Ferdinando gathered around him looked back to classical times for a complete wedding of words and music. The result was *Daphne*, composed by Jacopo

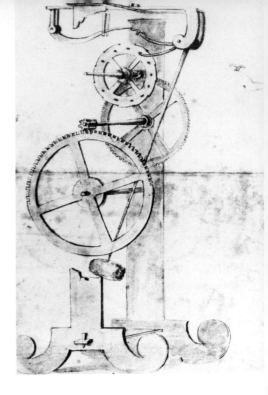

Corsi and Jacopo Peri to a libretto by Ottavio Rinussini; it was soon followed by *Euridice*, composed by Peri alone to another libretto by Rinussini. Each was performed before the court.

In 1609, Ferdinando was succeeded by his eldest son, Cosimo II, who was then nineteen. This amiable, tolerant ruler is now chiefly remembered for having been the patron of Galileo, with whom, before his accession, he had studied at Padua. Arrogant and sarcastic, Galileo had first been appointed professor of mathematics at Pisa, where he had swiftly antagonized his colleagues by his iconoclasm. Forced to resign, he had moved on to Padua in 1591. There, in one of the most enlightened centers of learning in the sixteenth-century world, he spent eighteen immensely fruitful and generally contented years. As soon as Cosimo became duke, he invited his former mentor, then forty-six years old, to come to Florence as his chief mathematician. Galileo's annual salary was to be 1,000 scudi, and Cosimo also made a villa at Arcetri available to him. Today everyone acknowledges the artistic brilliance of the Florentine legacy, but its scientific importance tends to be overlooked. Had it not been for the protection and encouragement of Cosimo II, Galileo's career might have been less glorious and even more troubled than it was. It is therefore fitting that he should have named the moons of Jupiter, which he discovered, the *Stellae Medicae* or *Medicea*.

Behind the villa of Poggio Imperiale, purchased by Cosimo's wife, the Grand Duchess Maria Maddalena, there rises the Torre del Galileo, which the scientist is believed to have used as his observatory during his years in Florence. Contrary to popular belief Galileo did not invent the telescope, and the instrument on display in the fascinating Museum of the Story of Science in Florence is not the first of its kind; but his brilliant deductions from his observations through this innovatory instrument make him, with Sir Isaac Newton, one of the two founders of the modern science of physics. Like Newton, he constructed most of his instruments himself, and did so with extraordinary ingenuity and skill.

Cosimo II died in 1620, at the early age of thirty, and was succeeded by his son, Ferdinando II, then only ten. According to Cosimo's will, his mother, Christine of Lorraine, and his wife, Maria Maddalena, sister of the Emperor Ferdinand II, were to act as regents until the new grand duke came of age. The prey of flattering courtiers and scheming prelates, these two women, stubborn but with no aptitude for affairs of state, proved powerless to check the corruption and inefficiency that began insidiously to undermine every department of government. And because they were also addicted to extravagant pomp and ceremony, they made serious inroads into the treasure that the more thrifty Cosimo had left in store in the Fortezza di San Giorgio. Thus began an inexorable decline in the power and prosperity of the Tuscan state, which was to continue long after the Medici had vanished from the scene.

In 1628, when he was only eighteen, Ferdinando dealt bravely and compassionately with another outbreak of the plague. He distributed money and food to the needy, set up isolation hospitals, and each day would make his way down from the comparative

Galileo, the greatest astronomer of the Renaissance, was a frail and nearly blind old man, broken and embittered by persecution and house arrest, when the English poet John Milton visited him in 1638. At the time Galileo, subject of this 1624 crayon drawing by Ottavio Leoni, was living in a tower on the outskirts of Florence. The tower, which still survives, served both as a celestial observatory and as a repository for the instruments and machines that Galileo made from diagrams like the one at left, which shows the works of a pendulum clock. Of the aged astronomer's searchings of the skies Milton wrote: "The moon whose orb/Through optic glass the Tuscan artist views/An evening from the top of Fiesole. . . ."

safety of San Giorgio, where the court had retreated, into the stench and heat of the city, in order to comfort and encourage his terrified subjects.

In his dealings concerning Galileo, Ferdinando showed less bravery. When, in 1633, the pope sent envoys to bring the scientist from Florence to Rome to face charges that he had gone back on a 1616 promise not to preach the heretical doctrine that the earth went around the sun instead of vice versa, Ferdinando and his grandmother tamely acquiesced. For this he has often been criticized by people who forget that he lived in an age when the majority of the people of Europe believed that a refusal to obey the command of the pope could result in eternal damnation. Again, when Ferdinando wished to raise a mausoleum to Galileo after the old man's death in 1642, he meekly submitted to an interdict of the Jesuits that he not do this and instead contented himself with seeing to it that the great scientist's body was interred in the Medici Chapel in Santa Croce.

After Ferdinando's grandmother died in 1636 he made an attempt to limit the powers of the church, to which she had given so much license and encouragement that it penetrated every nook and cranny of public and private life, destroying that spirit of free inquiry that had been the dominant characteristic of the High Renaissance. During this period, the Inquisition enjoyed total license in its enforcement of piety, prudery, and rigorous conformity or orthodoxy. The dreaded sessions of its court in the cloisters of Santa Croce were often followed by the burning of suspected heretics in the piazza without.

Ferdinando acquired, through his wife, Vittoria

della Rovere, the only surviving heir of the dukes of Urbino, a magnificent collection of paintings that included Titian's *Reclining Venus*, now in the Uffizi, and Raphael's portrait of Pope Julius II, with whom Michelangelo was so often at loggerheads, now in the Pitti Palace. To the Pitti he added two wings, each two stories high, and commissioned a number of the foremost artists of the day, among them Piero Berretini da Cortona and Ciro Ferri, to decorate them in a lavish, if uninspired, manner.

Two of the most durable achievements of his reign were the formation, with his brothers Giovanni Carlo and Leopold, of the Grand Ducal Library, the Palatina, which eventually provided the nucleus of the superb National Library, and the roofing in of the terraces of the Uffizi, to produce yet more space for the exhibition of the numerous valuable additions to the Medici collections made by the family.

One of Ferdinando's more eccentric actions was prompted by his desire to stimulate the declining agriculture of his domains: he introduced camels into Tuscany, to take the place of horses and oxen. Unfortunately, they did not thrive in the Italian climate and, in any case, the deeply conservative Tuscan peasantry did not take to the innovation. But descendants of these beasts can still be seen in Tenuta di San Rossore, once a grand ducal park and now a summer estate of the president of Italy.

Ferdinando was succeeded in 1670 by his son Cosimo III, who reigned for fifty-three years. The decline in the fortunes both of the Medici family and of the state, initiated by Ferdinando's amiable weak-

ness, was hastened by Cosimo's love of ostentation,
his extravagance, and his subordination to the twin
influences of his mother, the Grand Duchess Vittoria della Rovere, and the church. Corrupt clerics,
the Medici themselves, and a few of the leading families remained rich; but the people, misgoverned
and overtaxed, became poorer and poorer, with a
consequent decline in population—that of Florence
itself is estimated to have fallen below 50,000 by
1700—and a slow disintegration of buildings that no
one could afford to maintain.

It was during the reign of Cosimo III that the pi-
anoforte was invented in Florence in 1711 by Bartolommeo Cristofori; and it was Cosimo's librarian,
Antonio Magliabecchi, a hunchback so learned that
Mabillon wrote of him, *Ipse museum ambulans et viva
quaedam bibliotheca*—"He is himself a walking museum and a kind of living library," who collected the
immensely valuable manuscripts and codices known
at the Magliabecchian Library. But in general Cosimo III did little to revive the glories of Florence's
artistic and scientific past.

In this respect his son, Prince Ferdinando, was far
more effective. A brilliant and high-spirited young
man with a passion for music, art, and literature, he
was in constant opposition to the pompousness and
piety imposed on the court through the influence of
his grandmother Vittoria. He is credited with holding the first art exhibition, in the cloisters of Santa
Annunziata, in 1701; he himself directed produc-
tions of his plays in the little theater of his villa at
Pratolino; and he was also a composer of some skill.
Unfortunately, he predeceased his father.

Cosimo III's successor was therefore his second
son, Giovanni Gastone, who was fifty-two when, in
1723, he came to the throne. At first, he made a
number of promising reforms: the dismissal of the
more corrupt and inefficient of his father's advisers;
cuts in the taxes that had reduced so many of his
subjects to destitution; an amnesty for prisoners and
exiles; and a dismantling of the complex structure of
spies and informers that had created an atmosphere
of mutual suspicion throughout the duchy. But since
he too was childless, and since the only possible heir
to the throne was his sister Anna Maria Ludovica, he
was aware, even before his health began to decline
as a result of ceaseless dissipation, that both Austria
and Spain were preparing to claim Tuscany for their
own. At the Peace of Vienna in 1736 the great powers decided after some complex bargaining that on
the death of Giovanni Gastone the grand duchy
should go to Francis, duke of Lorraine, husband of
the Austrian emperor's daughter, Maria Theresa, in
return for his cession of Lorraine to the French.
Hearing this news, Giovanni Gastone lapsed into a
despair from which he never recovered.

The Electress Anna Maria Ludovica, last of the
Medici, was seventy when her brother died. A clev-
er, tough, and decisive woman, she had shown, both
during the twenty-four years she was married to the
Elector Palatinate of the Rhine and then, after the
elector's death, at the court of her father, that she
was far better fitted to govern Tuscany than her
brother, Giovanni Gastone, with whom she was seldom in agreement. But when Francis II first arrived
in Florence to claim his throne and then contemptu-

*"She lived retired," Horace Mann wrote of Anna
Maria Ludovica, last of the Medici, "but it was a
retirement of the utmost splendour. All that art and
ingenuity could supply and money could purchase the
aged daugher of Cosimo gathered round her—jewels,
precious metals, costly attire—the mass of these was
immense." At her death Anna Maria left all of the
Medici treasure, in toto and in perpetuity, to the state of
Tuscany—a bequest without equal in all of human
history. Through this act of unexampled beneficence the
aged daughter of Cosimo sought to express her family's
appreciation of their native city, an appreciation the city
has been less eager to reciprocate. No statue
commemorates Anna Maria's generosity, and no
Florentine street bears her name. Even the palazzo in
which she lived in utmost splendor does not bear her
family name alone. It is known as the Palazzo Medici-
Riccardi, and its courtyard is dominated by a soot-
begrimed statue of Orpheus by Baccio Bandinelli.*

ously appointed an agent, M. de Beauveu, to govern
it on his behalf, it became abundantly clear that she
would not have the opportunity to do so.

In a splendid act of generosity—which, in the
words of one Italian historian, "deserved to out-
weigh and make forgiven many faults of her ancestors"—this aged woman left all the Medici
possessions, estates, houses, chapels, works of art,
libraries, jewelry, and costumes, to the state of Tuscany forever, on condition that no part of this unparalleled bequest should ever be removed from
Florence and that it should be held for the benefit of
the public of all nations.

At a time when Florence had dwindled in financial
and political importance, when it had few factories,
and when it did not even possess a port to sustain
her, this was a truly magnificent patrimony. Even today, Florence survives largely through its visitors,
and those visitors would not throng the streets, fill
the hotels and restaurants to capacity, and buy from
its shops but for the former Medici possessions that
draw them there. The irony is that, whereas in London great families are everywhere commemorated,
the Medici, who did so much more for their city,
have only two minor streets named after them. Even
their former palace, sold by Ferdinand II in 1659,
has only recently come to be known as the Palazzo
Medici-Riccardi, instead of merely the Palazzo Riccardi.

The best epitaph for the remarkable Medici dynasty is probably that penned by Alexandre Dumas:
"They did more for the glory of the world than any
king, emperor or prince."

VII

Aftermath

The first Austrian grand duke, Francis II, entered the capital of his new dominion in 1738, through the Porta al Prato on the west side of Florence. The Cascine—once a hunting preserve of the Medici and today a public park held to be dangerous after nightfall—stretched beyond the Porta al Prato along the Arno. The event was marked by the erection of a triumphal arch between gate and park, an arch decorated with the flanking lions of the Republic, who seemed to frown at the arrival of the grand duke—and at the notion of the representative of one autocratic dynasty succeeding that of another. In general, however, the Austrian grand dukes were better rulers than the late Medici, theirs being the period of the Englightenment when absolutism tended to be tempered by benevolence. Thirty-five years after Francis II's accession, in 1773, the Society of Jesus was dissolved, but even before that date the terrors of the Inquisition and the corruption of ecclesiastical government had vanished from Florence.

Florence under the Austrian grand dukes has been described as a Garden of Eden, but an Eden without either the tree of knowledge or the tree of life. Leopold I, Ferdinand III, and Leopold II were all tolerant, efficient, and liberal-minded rulers. They systematized taxes and so made them more equitable; they encouraged agriculture, by then the foundation of the Tuscan economy, and inaugurated schemes of land reclamation; they threw open museums and galleries to the public; they built hospitals and poorhouses. Following the precepts of the Milanese reformer Giuseppe Beccaria, they even made theirs the first state in Europe to abolish the death penalty—something Great Britain was not to do until after World War II and the United States has yet to achieve. If in art and architecture they were maintainers rather than initiators, they can hardly be blamed. Although foreign artists of genius like Claude Lorrain and Nicolas Poussin might derive inspiration from their visits to Italy, it was only in Venice that the Italian artistic flame burned on effulgently. In Rome and Naples it emitted an occasional glow; in Florence it was extinct.

The Austrian grand dukes were temporarily ejected by Napoleon Bonaparte in 1796 when he conquered almost the whole of northern Italy with the assistance of Italians in sympathy with the aims of the French Revolution. Three years later Napoleon was dispossessed of most of this territory by the veteran Russian general Suvarov, a real-life character in Tolstoy's *War and Peace*, and by Cardinal Ruffo and his forces of Sanfedisti from Calabria. With his victory at Marengo the following year, however, the newly appointed first consul of France once more made himself master of Lombardy. And five years later the man who now called himself emperor of France won an even more decisive victory at Austerlitz, one that brought the whole of Italy, with the exception of Sicily and Sardinia, under his rule. The throne of Naples went first to his brother Joseph and then, in 1808, to his marshal, Joachim Murat. Of the rest of the peninsula, one area, designated the Kingdom of Italy, was put under the governorship of Napoleon's brother-in-law Eugène Beauharnais; yet another area, which included all of Tuscany, was annexed to France.

Unlike the English, the French stamped uniformity on the territories they conquered and in this respect Italy was no exception. Small, separate states, all with differing forms of government, differing penal systems, and their own armies and customs barriers, were now rigidly integrated. The Code Napoleon, so far ahead of most other legal systems in its liberality, and the metric system, so much more convenient for commerce, were everywhere imposed—and in this sense it might be said by conquering Italy Napoleon did as much to unite it as did Giuseppi Mazzini, Giuseppi Garibaldi, or the conte di Cavour, the great heroes of the nineteenth-century Risorgimento. Even Napoleon's ruthless conscription of Italians into the Grande Armée, where many met their deaths, and his promiscuous looting of their art treasures had the effect of uniting them, if only in common detestation and fear.

As a result, when Ferdinand III returned to his duchy after the defeat of Napoleon and the subsequent Congress of Vienna in 1815, he found that his position had, paradoxically, been rendered not more but less secure. The kind of benevolent paternalism that had marked his rule was already out of date. Secret societies dedicated to the establishment of a liberal constitution came into being in Florence, as they did in the other major cities of Italy.

In 1848, the year of revolutions, uprisings compelled Leopold II to grant the Florentines a constitution under a radical ministry that included such men as Guerrazzi, Montanelli, Mazzini, and Prince Corsini-Lajatico, a member of the famous family whose superb seventeenth-century palace fronts the Lung' Arno. Despite these concessions, the grand duke was obliged to flee Florence in 1849, leaving Guerrazzi to rule in his stead. Recalled a mere fortnight later in circumstances of typically Italian confusion and political rivalry, Leopold II arrived in the city with 10,000 Austrian soldiers and at once abolished the constitution and resumed his absolutist rule. By 1859, however, he had come to realize that the Italian desire for unity and freedom was so potent he had no course but to abdicate.

The ardor, dissension, and extravagant hope of these years and those that immediately followed them—years in which the French emperor Napoleon III often playing a characteristically tricky part—are mirrored in the poems of Elizabeth Barrett Browning. She and her husband had taken up residence in Casa Guidi, a stone's throw from the Pitti Palace; and it is above all her collection of poems *From Casa Guidi Windows* that resurrects that time for English and American readers. She often seems as passionately devoted to the French emperor as to the cause of freedom, and in both these attachments—as in her attachment to spiritualism—her husband tends to lag behind her.

The lives of this couple—in Pisa, Rome, and, especially, in Florence—are typical of those of the many distinguished foreign visitors who, for shorter or longer periods were then making Italy their home. Because Mrs. Browning was world-famous, and her husband scarcely less so, by the time they settled in Florence in 1847, they were sought out by everyone of prominence. Frederick Tennyson, brother of the poet laureate and himself a poet of

some distinction; Lord Lytton, a grandee who was to become English ambassador in Paris and then the viceroy of India; Nathaniel Hawthorne, who stayed at the Torre di Montauto, between Bellosguardo, present seat of the American School of Florence, and Soffiano; James Russell Lowell; Harriet Beecher Stowe (of whom Elizabeth Browning wrote in a letter, "Never did a lioness roar more softly"); Walter Savage Landor: these were some of the people who came and went in what Mrs. Browning described as "a little dream-life, where if ever one is over-busy, the old tapestries on the walls and the pre-Giotto pictures surround us, ready to quiet us again."

Many of these prominent foreigners came to Florence not merely in search of the quiet provided by tapestries and pictures but also, like Mrs. Browning herself, in search of health—and in this second quest they were rarely successful. In the Protestant Cemetery in Florence, once a retreat far from the dust and din of the city, but now surrounded by highways foul and noisy with cars, among the graves of such people as Arthur Hugh Clough, who fretted himself to a shadow in unrequited love for Florence Nightingale, and those of both Walter Savage Landor and Mrs. Browning herself, there are innumerable tombstones that record the deaths of totally unremarkable foreigners. Many of these died in their teens or early twenties, and one cannot help but think that the notorious climate of Florence, cruelly hot and humid in summer and cold and dank in winter, must have speeded, rather than retarded, the inroads of the pulmonary consumption from which many of them were suffering.

In 1868, seven years after the death of Mrs. Browning—"smilingly, happily, with a face like a girl's," as her husband put it—Feodor Dostoyevsky paid a visit to Florence, staying less than fifty yards from the house of Paolo dal Pozzo Toscanelli, the great fifteenth-century geographer, and less than two hundred yards from Casa Guidi. It was at No. 21 Piazza Pitti that the Russian novelist, often suffering several epilepitc fits in a single week, wrote much of *The Idiot*. It is a pity that he and Browning, by then back in England, did not meet, since a confrontation between two such different geniuses could only have been interesting; and it is a pity that Browning's great friend Landor did not live long enough to give us one of his *Imaginary Conversations* between them.

Landor lived in Florence, off and on, for an immensely long period. By 1821 he was already lodging in rooms in the Palazzo Medici-Riccardi, where he was visited by William Hazlitt. Six years later he acquired the Villa Gherardesca, on a hillside below Fiesole, which he renamed Villa Landor. Violent conflicts with both his wife and his neighbors prevented him from full enjoyment of this idyllic spot, with its fine views of Valdarno and Vallombrosa. It was in this villa that Landor, furious with a cook who had ruined a dish, hurled him from a first-floor window—only to stammer out, aghast, "Good God, I forgot the violets!" It was, however, in Via Nunziata in Florence that Algernon Swinburne visited him; and it was there that he died in 1864, obstinate, quarrelsome, and courageous to the last.

The two Victorians who had the most influence in drawing pilgrims to Florence, as to an artistic Lor-etto or Fatima, were the Englishman John Ruskin with *Mornings in Florence* and the Swiss Jacob Burckhardt with *The Civilisation of the Renaissance in Italy*. But whatever their nationality, these eminent visitors were more interested in the Florence of the past than of the present. When we read their books, letters, and diaries we realize that all of their spiritual communion was with buildings, statues, pictures, and views—and all of their social communication, with few exceptions, was with each other. As a result, the foreigners stand out like principals in an opera. Florentines merely provide a shadowy chorus behind them. The majority of houses in certain streets—for example, those set back among extensive gardens in the Via S. Leonardo, in one of the more humble of which, No. 64, Pietr Tchaikovsky lodged in 1878—were often occupied by foreigners.

Soon after the publication of Burckhardt's masterpiece in 1860, Tuscany ceased to be an independent state and merged into a united Italy. In 1864 Florence succeeded Turin as capital of the newly founded kingdom, but after five brief years it was obliged to cede this honor to Rome. After that, in the words of the late Victorian travel writer and artist Augustus Hare, Florence "sunk into a mere provincial city, bereft of the presence of a court and paying more than six times the amount of taxes it paid under the Grand Dukes."

The reigns of King Vittorio Emmanuele and his successors brought with them the sometimes dubious benefits of progress. So that wide boulevards could be constructed, the third circle of walls that girded Florence was ruthlessly pulled down. Worse

still, the accretions of two thousand years of history were swept away so that the Piazza Vittorio Emmanuele and the streets around it could be erected in all their empty grandeur. The people who had lived in this area, once regarded as a slum, were relocated, usually against their will, in new housing especially built for them outside the Porta San Frediano.

In the center of this new square was set up a bronze equestrian statue of King Vittorio Emmanuele III, with a triumphal arch behind it, and in the surrounding streets were built the kind of houses that Browning had in mind when he wrote:

> They are stone-faced, white as a curd, there's
>   something to take the eye!
> Houses in four straight lines not a single front awry!
> Green blinds as a matter of course, to draw when the
>   sun gets high,
> And the shops with fanciful signs which are painted
>   properly.

What seemed to some appalling vandalism and to others an urgent act of slum clearance—defended by a mayor of the time with the defiant statement "Florence belongs not to the *forestieri* [visitors] but to the Florentines, and the Florentines may do as they please"—typifies a conflict that continues to the present. Visitors and those natives of the city who are rich enough to live in tastefully modernized apartments or houses deplore the destruction of an ancient inheritance. Reformers and those who have to endure the dampness, the dilapidation, and the overcrowding of what are, to them, merely picturesque hovels insist that the old must make way for

the new. It is only unfortunate that the new in Florence should, as in many other cities, be so often depressingly undistinguished and even gimcrack. What modern Italian architects are capable of producing is demonstrated by the thrilling Stadio Communale at Campo di Marte, designed in 1932 by Pier Luigi Nervi, an architect-engineer in the tradition of Arnolfo di Cambio and Brunelleschi; but much of their work in Florence is timidly derivative, as though they had been overawed—as well they might be—by the glories of the past.

Those twentieth-century visitors who settled in Florence before World War II tended to do so not in search of health but of cheap living—and, in some cases, of sexual freedom and tolerance. Typical of the first category were the widows, spinsters, and retired couples who found it easier to eke out pensions abroad than at home. Typical of the second category were a number of writers. There was, for example, Ouida (Marie Louise de la Ramée), whose affair with an Italian nobleman had led her to engage her rival, an English *grande dame* named Janet Ross, in a slanging match from their carriages in the Via Tornabuoni—much to the scandalized amusement of all who witnessed or heard of it. There was Norman Douglas, who had been obliged to quit England hurriedly after making an indiscreet offer to a schoolboy met in the Natural History Museum in London. There was Oscar Wilde's friend and supporter Reginald Turner, an unsuccessful novelist, who, when he heard Somerset Maugham boasting about the prices that second-hand copies of his books were fetching, retorted: "*My* most valuable

In an act more churlish than strategic, the retreating Germans dynamited all of the Arno bridges—save only the Ponte Vecchio—when they abandoned Florence at the end of World War II. The gesture was otiose, however, for the Allies lost no time in erecting temporary bridges, crossing the Arno, and pursuing the Axis troops northward. This Associated Press photograph shows the wreckage of Ponte Santa Trinita as its ruined piers are leveled by British dynamite charges to make way for a Bailey bridge. (The undamaged Ponte Vecchio is visible at the rear.) In the immediate postwar period Santa Trinita was rebuilt precisely as Ammanati planned it, using his original plans and many of the original stones.

editions are my second ones. They just cannot be found." There was Lady Troubridge, who fled from the rough embraces of her admiral husband to the welcoming bosom of the novelist Radcliffe Hall, author of the once-notorious *The Well of Loneliness.*

At the close of the war, the retreating Germans blew up all of Florence's bridges but the Ponte Vecchio, with the result that visitors arriving soon after the cessation of hostilities were obliged to pick their way over heaps of rubble, from which the wind often raised a thick, suffocating dust. The German action was totally pointless: the Allied armies threw new bridges across the Arno in a matter of days, and in any case, there was no chance that the tiny German force that occupied Florence at the close of the war, by then detested by their former allies, could put up an effective resistance.

The bridges were rebuilt, the Ponte S. Trinita exactly as Ammanati had planned it—from his original designs and with the same kind of tools, using either the original stones recovered from the Arno or ones precisely like them brought from the old quarries above the Boboli Gardens. For a time the head of one of the statues, the *Primavera*, could not be found, and dark rumors circulated among the Florentines that a colonel of the American Occupation had sneaked it home in his luggage. But when the Parker Pen Company, wishing either to gain favorable publicity for itself or to save the United States from unfavorable publicity, offered a $3,000 reward to anyone who produced the head, it was eventually recovered in extensive dredging operations. The neighborhoods at either end of the Ponte Vecchio

fared less happily, being reconstructed in a style that is an uneasy compromise between old and new. Viewed from either bank of the Arno, they fail to convince the eye that they are in integral part of an otherwise beautiful riverscape.

Worse than any damage caused by the Germans was that inflicted by floods in 1966. Torrential rain began to fall on the eve of the annual holiday that celebrates Italy's victory in World War I, November 1. Soon the water level had risen to ten feet in the Piazza del Duomo; families were marooned on the tops of buildings, awaiting rescue by helicopter; and dead animals, smashed furniture, and uprooted trees were being whirled along on the irresistible tide. Even worse than this first devastation was the legacy of mud, fuel oil, and burst sewers the flood waters left behind. Hotels, restaurants, and cafés closed, trains did not run, the highways were impassable. Shops lost all their merchandise to the rapacious tide, and in its wake the foundations of ancient buildings were dangerously eroded, priceless frescoes were smeared with mud and slime, and ancient manuscripts and books disintegrated, often beyond repair. FIRENZE INVASA DALLE ACQUE, a newspaper headline ran, *La Città transformata in un lago*— "FLORENCE SWEPT BY FLOODS, The city transformed into a lake." Reports appeared in the foreign press that typhoid and even cholera had broken out, but these, fortunately, were not true.

In her wonderfully vivid diary of these events, *Florence: Ordeal by Water*, Kathrine Kressman Taylor describes the heroism of the Florentines in saving not merely what they could of their own personal

129

*Florentines treasure the past, but they live in the present—
and their vital presence is an essential part of the
impression any visitor carries away with him. Because they
are mindful of their remarkable heritage, Florentines
preserve it through painstaking restoration (top right).
Because they appreciate that their city is a cynosure, not a
cenotaph, they savor its immediate pleasures—such as
rowing on the Arno (directly above)—as well as its
unparalleled artistic attractions.*

131

possessions but also threatened works of art. Typical were employees of the Uffizi who, in her words, "breasted the climbing flood to reach the galleries, some of them striving for two hours to cross the torrents in the streets, and who laboured without rest or food for a long day and night to save masterpieces . . . from the waters. . . ."

Soon hundreds of people, many of them foreign students, were pouring into the city to give their help in the immense task of reclamation and repair. All were impressed by the grimly humorous stoicism with which the Florentines accepted a tragedy that, in many cases, had simultaneously ruined their homes and their very livelihoods. Amazingly enough, there are now few indications of this recent devastation, other than the signs on many famous buildings that the 1966 flood waters came up to this or that mark. The only difference between the flood of 1333 and this flood is that, on the latter occasion, not only Florence but the whole world was concerned for the fate of the city.

The most famous foreign resident of Florence in our own time was the art historian Bernard Berenson. Having amassed a vast fortune by acting as adviser, in an increasingly uneasy relationship, to that prince of art dealers, Lord Duveen, Berenson settled in his magnificent villa, I Tatti, in Settignano. In his last years, especially after World War II—during which, as a Jew, he had eventually been obliged to go into hiding—he occupied the position of uncrowned monarch of the city, with a small but reverential court to which museums, libraries, and dealers would send their reverential ambassadors.

In the Commedia *Dante refers to the Arno, which bisects his native city from west to east, as* il bel fiume—*"the beautiful river." But being, like all Florentines, of two minds about the river, he also calls it* la maladetta e sventurata fossa—*"the cursed and luckless ditch." In November 1966, autumnal rains were to transform the beautiful river into a swollen torrent and lead luckless Florence to curse Dante's ditch. By the time the flood waters subsided, the city had been buried in slime and many of its invaluable art works had been defaced or destroyed. Bas-reliefs were scoured from the sides of the Duomo, and several panels of the Baptistery doors were carried away. Muck and mire filled the square in front of Santa Croce (far left, below) and roiling water swirled through the Uffizi archives, leaving precious manuscripts hopelessly waterlogged (near left). One measure of how high the angry waters rose is the photograph at far left, which shows waterborne debris clinging to the second story of the Ponte Vecchio—and gaping holes below, where the famed goldsmiths' shops had once stood.*

OVERLEAF: The light of Tuscany is always magical, but never more so than at dusk, when its deepening amber begins to yield to the artificial lighting of the city.

An increasingly frail octogenarian and then nonagenarian, he would rouse himself and totter out, like some living relic of aestheticism sought out in worship, to greet yet another busload of tourists who would wave, stare, and click their cameras at him. His influence on the way the world looked at Italian art and the prices it paid for that art was more potent than that of any of his contemporaries, and many are the stories of the delicacy of sensibilities that later replaced what had once been a real toughness in the marketplace. According to one story, Berenson's manservant would be obliged each morning to warm his wristwatch so that the touch of metal should not administer too violent a shock to his skin. Yet, sadly, this supreme proponent of style was cruelly fretted by the consciousness that, despite his friendships with such writers as Edith Wharton and Logan Pearsall Smith (whose sister he married), and despite the help he received from such colleagues as Kenneth Clark and Raymond Mortimer, his own style remained turgid and graceless.

Those who knew Florence before World War II or even in the early years after it often complain of the present noise, the crowds, and the stink of petrol fumes. As far as the complaint of crowds is concerned, it is one that foreign visitors, on the priniciple "I am a traveler; *you* are a tourist," have been making for generations. As far as the complaint of noise is concerned, Berenson himself once remarked to this author that it was every whit as bad when horse- and ox-drawn carts creaked and clattered over the cobbles, street-hawkers constantly bellowed word of their wares, and women carried on animated conversations from one window to another over the heads of passersby below. But cars certainly present a new and particularly virulent nuisance, as do motor scooters—from which Italians often remove the mufflers so that they can announce their passing with even more éclat. It is odd that the municipality, unlike those of other major Italian cities, should have been so timid in establishing the traffic-free zone it *has* demarcated—and then in enforcing the prohibition.

Through Florence the tourists—both famous and unknown—pass, as they have for centuries, each with exclamations of wonder, pleasure, disappointment, annoyance, and astonishment. Goethe was chiefly impressed not by the art and architecture but by the efficiency of the roads and bridges. Samuel Rogers, author of a number of poems about Italy but now chiefly remembered as the entertainer of other poets at breakfast, remarked of Michelangelo's *Lorenzo* that "it fascinates and is intolerable." Ruskin dismissed the monuments to the greatness of Florence in Santa Croce as "the paltriest of all possible sculpture, trying to be grand by bigness and pathetic by expense." Swinburne's melodramatic verdict on Andrea del Sarto was that "His life was corroded by the poisonous solvent of love, and his soul was burnt into dead ashes." What most pleased Dostoycvsky in Florence was the reading room where he could pore over the Russian papers.

Such judgments are largely ephemeral and they often contradict each other. Florence, rising up in defiance of the inroads of war, floods, and visitors, is permanent and reconciles all contradictions.

133

FLORENCE IN LITERATURE

"Oh, ungrateful country, what madness, what forgetfulness possessed thee, when with unaccustomed cruelty thou didst put to flight thy dearest citizen, thine eminent benefactor, thine only poet? Or what possessed thee subsequently? If, perchance, thou excusest thyself by the general madness of the moment, induced by evil counsel, why, when anger had passed away, and tranquillity of mind was restored, didst thou not repent of the deed and recall him." Thus did one of Florence's most famous sons—the storyteller Boccaccio—write in the mid-fourteenth century about another famous son of Florence—Dante. The madness to which Boccaccio referred was civil war, one in which Dante found himself accused of graft and exiled from the city of his birth. In all his long banishment, which was to last twenty years, Dante never abandoned hope that his supreme triumph, The Divine Comedy, *would reopen the city's gates to him. But Florence never repented, and Dante died in exile at the age of fifty-six, leaving behind these bittersweet lines from the* Commedia.

If ever it happen that the sacred song
   Whereto both heaven and earth have set a hand,
   Whereby I am lean, these many years and long,
O'ercome the cruelty which keeps me banned
   From the fair sheepfold where I slept, a lamb,
   Foe to the wolves that raven through the land.
With different voice now, not with fleece the same,
   Shall I return, poet, and at the fount
   Of my baptizing shall the chaplet claim,
Because into the faith that makes the account
   Of souls to God I won then; for which worth
   Peter wreathed such a light about my front.
Thereafter toward us moved a splendour forth
   Out of that sphere whence we had seen issue
   The first fruits of Christ's vicars left on earth.
Whereon my Lady, full of gladness new,
   Said to me: "Look; look! see the Baron move
   For whose sake is Galicia journeyed to."
As when by its companion comes a dove
   To settle close, and each one to its mate,
   Turning and cooing, poureth forth its love,
So the one prince, so glorious and great,
   I saw received by the other, while that food
   They lauded, spread above, their souls to sate.
But when the welcome was complete, they stood
   Each of them silent *coram me*, so bright
   And burning that my sight was all subdued.
Smiling then, Beatrice spoke: "Illustrious light,
   To whom 'twas given the bounteous largess
   Of our celestial palace once to write.
Do thou make Hope to sound in this high place:
   Thou knowest that thou as often hast pictured it
   As Jesus showed the three that special grace."
"Lift up thy head, and confidently quiet
   Thyself! For whatso mortal dares to soar
   Hither, our rays must ripen and complete."
The second flame this comfort breathed: wherefore
   I lifted up mine eyes unto the hills

Which beat them down by too much weight before.
"Since, ere death, of His grace our Emperor wills
   That face to face thou should'st His Nobles see
   In the most secret hall His presence fills,
That having seen this Court in verity
   Thou is thyself and others mayest breed
   Stronger the hope on earth enamouring thee,
Say what this is, and how therewith the seed
   Flowers in thy mind; and say whence comes this thing."
   Thus further did the second light proceed;
And that compassionate one who set my wing,
   Guiding its feathers, on a flight so vast,
   Fore-ran my answer, herself thus answering:
"Church Militant hath not a child to boast
   Of greater hope; 'tis writ in the Sun's beam
   Which radiateth over all our host.
Therefore from Egypt to Jerusalem
   'Twas granted him to come, to look on her,
   Before his soldier's service end for him.
The other two points asked by thee, which were
   Not for the sake of knowing, but to record
   How much this virtue to thy heart is dear,
I leave to him; for they will not be hard,
   Nor theme for vain-glory: let him reply
   Therefore, and God this grace to him accord."
Like pupil answering teacher eagerly,
   Prompt in those points wherein he is most expert,
   To give proof of his quality, "Hope," said I,
"Is certain expectation that the heart
   Has of the future glory; the effect
   Of divine grace and precedent desert.
Me did the light from many stars direct;
   He first distilled it into me with his breath,
   Singer supreme of the supreme Prefect.
For 'let them put their trust in thee' he saith
   In his psalm, 'all who know thy name'; and who
   Knoweth it not, if he possess my faith?
Then didst thou into me instil his dew
   In thine epistle, so that I overflow
   And upon others spill your rain anew."
While I was speaking, a quick-throbbing glow
   In that fire's living bosom was revealed,
   Like lightning in its sudden come-and-go.
Then spoke its breath: "The warm love still not quelled
   For that dear virtue, which companioned me
   Even to the palm and the issue of the field,
Bids me breathe to thee, who find'st felicity
   In her; and me it pleases that thou tell
   What thing it is that Hope has promised thee."

DANTE
The Divine Comedy, c. 1320

Giovanni Boccaccio's Life of Dante—*although written sometime between 1353, the year he finished a collection of anecdotes and tales known as* The Decameron, *and 1373, the year he gave his first public lectures on Dante in Florence—was not printed until more than a century later, when it appeared as prefatory material in a Venetian edition of* The Divine Comedy. *Only eight at the time of Dante's death, Boccaccio nevertheless felt a special literary kinship with the banished poet, and he doggedly assembled the materials for his* Life *in the face of public antipathy and in the absence of any published sources. The result was not only the first of many biographies of the greatest of all Renaissance poets but also one of the first genuinely modern biographies ever written.*

Florence, as well as the other most noble Italian cities, took her beginning from the Romans, as the ancient histories tell us and as the common opinion of people now runs. In provess of time she grew larger, became full of people and of illustrious citizens, and began to appear to her neighbors not merely a city but a power. Whether the ultimate cause of the change was adverse fortune, or the ill-will of heaven, or the deserts of her citizens, is uncertain; but it is clear that, not many centuries after, Attila, the cruel king of the Vandals, and the general devastator of nearly all Italy, killed and dispersed all or the greater part of her citizens who were famous for noble blood or for other reasons, and reduced Florence itself to ashes and ruins. Thus it remained, it is believed, for more than three hundred years. At the end of that time the imperial power of Rome was transferred, not without cause, from Greece to Gaul; and Charles the Great, then the most clement king of the French, was raised to the imperial throne. After many labors, moved, I believe, by the divine spirit, he turned his imperial mind to the rebuilding of this desolate city; and although he limited its size by a small circuit of walls, he had it rebuilt, so far as he could, after the likeness of Rome, and settled by those who had been its first founders, collecting inside the walls, nevertheless, the few remnants which could be found of the descendants of the ancient exiles.

Among these new inhabitants—perhaps one who superintended the rebuilding, or assigned the houses and streets, or gave to this new people the necessary laws—there came from Rome, as the story runs, a noble youth of the family of the Frangipani, called by all Eliseo. He, by chance, after he had accomplished the principal purpose for which he was come, became a permanent resident of the city, drawn either by love for the city which he had so recently helped to reorganize; or by the pleasant site, to which he perhaps saw that heaven in future must be favorable; or by some other cause. After him he left a large and worthy family of sons and descendants, who, abandoning the ancient surname of their ancestors, took for a surname that of him who had founded their family, and all called themselves the Elisei. As time went on and son succeeded father, there was born and lived, in this family, a brave knight, remarkable for his deeds and his wisdom, whose name was Cacciaguida. To him, in his youth, was given by his elders as bride a damsel born of the Aldighieri of Ferrara, esteemed for her beauty and character as well as for her noble blood, with whom he lived many years, and by whom he had many children. Whatever the others were called, it pleased the mother to revive for one the name of her ancestors, as women are wont to like to do, naming him Aldighieri, although the word afterwards, dropping the letter *d*, became Alighieri. The worth of this man brought it about that all who descended from him forsook the name of Elisei, and called themselves Alighieri—a practice which has lasted to our time. From here were descended many children, and great-grandchildren, and, in the reign of the Emperor Frederick the Second, one whose name was Alighieri, and who was destined to become illustrious through his son rather than by himself. His wife, when with child and not far distant from the time of parturition, saw in a dream what the fruit of her womb should be; and the dream is now clear to all, although it was not then understood by her or by others.

It seemed to the gentle lady in her dream that she was under a lofty laurel tree in a green meadow, hard by a clear spring, and here she felt herself give birth to a son, who, in a brief space of time, feeding only upon the berries which fell from the laurel tree, and drinking of the waters of the clear spring, seemed to her to become a shepherd, and to strive with all his might to lay hold on the leaves of the laurel tree whose fruit had fed him. And in striving for this, he seemed to her to fall, and on rising to have become no more a man but a peacock. At this she was so greatly astonished that she awoke, and not a long while after the proper time came for her labor, and she gave birth to a son, to whom she and his father gave by common consent the name of Dante; and appropriately, too, since, as we shall see later, the result fitted the name excellently. This was that Dante of whom I write; this was that Dante who was granted to our age by the special grace of God; that was that Dante who first was destined to open the way for the return to Italy of the banished Muses. By him the glory of the Florentine idiom was made manifest; by him all the beauties of the common speech were set to fitting numbers; by him dead poetry may properly be said to have been revived. These things, if fittingly considered, will show that he could have rightly had no other name than Dante.

GIOVANNI BOCCACCIO
Life of Dante, c. 1373

LORENZO THE MAGNIFICENT

Niccolo Machiavelli was born in Florence in 1469, the last year of Piero de Medici's benevolent administration, and he was but a child when the Pazzi Conspiracy attempted to thwart the succession of Lorenzo de Medici. Both Lorenzo and Niccolo Machiavelli survived those turbulent times—the former to establish a family dynasty that would reshape the history of Florence, the latter to transcribe that history. Machiavelli is best known today as the author of The Prince, *the first treatise on the role of the modern autocrat—a work dedicated, quite appropriately, to that modern autocrat Lorenzo de Medici. But Machiavelli also wrote a history of Florence that draws upon the events of his childhood and presents Lorenzo in a more complex and more flattering light.*

In the meantime, the whole city was roused to arms, and Lorenzo de' Medici, accompanied by a numerous escort, returned to his house. The palace was recovered from its assailants, all of whom were either slain or made prisoners. The name of the Medici echoed everywhere, and portions of dead bodies were seen borne on spears and scattered through the streets; whilst every one was transported with rage against the Pazzi, and pursued them with relentless cruelty. . . .

The changes desired by the pope and the king, in the government of

Florence, not having taken place, they determined to effect by war what they had failed to accomplish by treachery; and both assembled forces with all speed to attack the Florentine states; publicly declaring, that they only wished the citizens to remove Lorenzo de' Medici, who alone of all the Florentines was their enemy. The king's forces had already passed the Tronto, and the pope's were in Perugia; and that the citizens might feel the effect of spiritual as well as temporal weapons, the pontiff excommunicated and anathematized them. Finding themselves attacked by so many armies, the Florentines prepared for their defense with the utmost care. Lorenzo de' Medici, as the enemy's operations were said to be directed against himself alone, resolved first of all to assemble the Signory, and the most influential citizens, in the palace, to whom, being above three hundred in number, he spoke as follows:—"Most excellent signors, and you, magnificent citizens, I know not whether I have more occasion to weep with you for the events which have recently occurred, or to rejoice in the circumstances with which they have been attended. Certainly, when I think with what virulence of united deceit and hatred I have have been attacked, and my brother murdered, I cannot but mourn and grieve from my heart, from my very soul. Yet when I consider with what promptitude, anxiety, love, and unanimity of the whole city my brother has been avenged and myself defended, I am not only compelled to rejoice, but feel myself honored and exalted; for if experience has shown me that I had more enemies than I apprehended, it has also proved that I possess more warm friends than I could ever have hoped for. I must therefore grieve with you for the injuries others have suffered, and rejoice in the attachment you have exhibited towards myself; but I feel more aggrieved by the injuries committed, since they are so unusual, so unexampled, and (as I trust you believe) so undeserved on our part. Think, magnificent citizens, to what a dreadful point ill fortune has reduced our family, when amongst friends, amidst our own relatives, nay, in God's holy temple, we have found our greatest foes. Those who are in danger turn to their friends for assistance; they call upon their relatives for aid; but we found ours armed, and resolved on our destruction. Those who are persecuted, either from public or private motives, flee for refuge to the altars; but where others are safe, we are assassinated; where parricides and assassins are secure, the Medici find their murderers. But God, who has not hitherto abandoned our house, again saved us, and has undertaken the defense of our just cause. What injury have we done to justify so intense desire of our own destruction? Certainly those who have shown themselves so much our enemies, never received any private wrong from us; for, had we wished to injure them, they would not have had an opportunity of injuring us. If they attribute public grievances to ourselves (supposing any had been done to them) they do the greater injustice to you, to this palace, to the majesty of this government, by assuming that on our account you would act unfairly to any of your citizens; and such a supposition, as we all know, is contradicted by every view of the circumstances; for we, had we been able, and you, had we wished it, would never have contributed to so abominable a design. Whoever inquires into the truth of these matters, will find that our family has always been exalted by you, and from this sole cause, that we have endeavored by kindness, liberality, and beneficence, to do good to all; and if we have

honored strangers, when did we ever injure our relatives? If our enemies' conduct has been adopted, to gratify their desire of power (as would seem to be the case from their having taken possession of the palace and brought an armed force into the piazza) the infamous, ambitious, and destestable motive is at once disclosed. If they were actuated by envy and hatred of our authority, they offend you rather than us; for from you we have derived all the influence we possess. Certainly usurped power deserves to be detested; but not distinctions conceded for acts of kindness, generosity, and magnificence. And you all know that our family never attained any rank to which this palace and your united consent did not raise it. Cosmo, my grandfather, did not return from exile with arms and violence, but by your unanimous desire and approbation. It was not my father, old and infirm, who defended the government against so many enemies, but yourselves by your authority and benevolence defended him; neither could I, after his death, being then a boy, have maintained the position of my house except by your favor and advice. Nor should we ever be able to conduct the affairs of this republic, if you did not contribute to our support. Therefore, I know not the reason of their hatred towards us, or what just cause they have of envy. Let them direct their enmity, against their own ancestors, who, by their pride and avarice, lost the reputation which ours, by very opposite conduct, were enabled to acquire. But let it be granted we have greatly injured them, and that they are justified in seeking our ruin; why do they come and take possession of the palace? Why enter into league with the pope and the king, against the liberties of this republic? Why break the long-continued peace of Italy? They have no excuse for this; they ought to confine their vengeance to those who do them wrong, and not confound private animosities with public grievances. Hence it is that since their defeat our misfortune is the greater; for on their account the pope and the king make war upon us, and this war, they say, is directed against my family and myself. And would to God that this were true; then the remedy would be sure and unfailing, for I would not be so base a citizen as to prefer my own safety to yours; I would at once resolve to ensure your security, even though my own destruction were the immediate and inevitable consequence. But as the wrongs committed by princes are usually concealed under some less offensive covering, they have adopted this plea to hide their more abominable purposes. If, however, you think otherwise, I am in your hands; it is with you to do with me what you please. You are my fathers, my protectors, and whatever you command me to do I will perform most willingly; nor will I ever refuse, when you find occasion to require it, to close the war with my own blood which was commenced with that of my brother." Whilst Lorenzo spoke, the citizens were unable to refrain from tears, and the sympathy with which he had been heard was extended to their reply, delivered by one of them in the name of the rest, who said that the city acknowledged many advantages derived from the good qualities of himself and his family; and encouraged him to hope that with as much promptitude as they had used in his defense . . . they would secure to him his influence in the government which he should never lose whilst they retained possession of the country.

NICCOLO MACHIAVELLI
History of Florence, 1503

No one would deny that the artifacts created by Benvenuto Cellini, master goldsmith and sculptor of the Florentine High Renaissance, are anything less than masterpieces, but it may well be that Cellini's greatest gift to posterity is not wrought of precious metals but written on parchment. His racy, vividly detailed autobiography, begun in 1588 and first published in 1730, is one of the great documents of the epoch and one of the great autobiographies of all time. Dictated initially to an apprentice goldsmith, it casts Cellini himself in a role of exaggerated importance in the contemporary events it describes, but it also marks the emergence of modern individualism, the great legacy of the Renaissance.

My name, then, is Benvenuto Cellini, and I am the son of Maestro Giovanni, the son of Andrea, the son of Cristofano Cellini; my mother was Maria Lisabetta, daughter to Stefano Granacci: and both my parents were citizens of Florence. It appears from the ancient chronicles compiled by natives of that city, men highly deserving of credit, that it was built after the model of Rome. This is evident from the vestiges of the Colosseum, and the hot baths, near the Holy Cross: the capitol was an ancient market-place: the rotunda, which is still entire, was built for a temple of Mars, and is now called San Giovanni's church. This is so evident that it cannot be denied; but the above-mentioned structures are of much smaller dimensions than those of Rome. It is said that they were erected by Julius Caesar, in conjunction with some other Roman patricians, who, having subdued and taken Fiesole, in this very place founded a city, and each of them undertook to erect one of these remarkable edifices. Julius Caesar had a very gallant officer of the first rank in his army, named Florentius of Cellino, which is a castle within two miles of Monte Fiascone: this Florentius having taken up his quarters under Fiesole, where Florence at present stands, to be near the river Arno for the conveniences of his army, all the soldiers and others who had any business with that officer used to say, "Let us go to Florence;" as well because the name of the officer was Florentius, as because on the spot where he had fixed his headquarters there was great plenty of flowers. Thus in the infancy of the town, the elegant appellation of Florence seeming to Julius Caesar appropriate, and its allusion to flowers appearing auspicious, he gave it the name of Florentia; at the same time paying a compliment to his valiant officer, to whom he was the more attached, because he had promoted him from a very humble station, and considered his merit as in some measure a creation of his own. The other name of *Fluentia*, which the learned inventors and investigators of the connexion of names pretend that Florence obtained on account of the Arno's *flowing* through the town, cannot be admitted; because the Tiber flows through Rome, the Po through Ferrara, the Saone through Lyons, the Seine through Paris, which cities have various names, no way derived from the course of those rivers. I believe the matter to be as I have stated, and am of opinion that this city takes its name from the valiant captain Florentius.

I have also learned that there are some of our family of Cellini in Ravenna, a much more ancient city than Florence, and that they are people of quality: there are also some of the family in Pisa, and in several other parts of Christendom; besides a few families that still remain in Tuscany. Most of these have been devoted to arms. It is not many years since a beardless youth, of the name of Luca Cellini, encountered a most valiant and practised soldier, named Francesco da Vicorati, who had often

fought in the lists: Luca, who had only courage on his side, vanquished and slew him; envincing such prowess and intrepidity as astonished the spectators, who all expected a contrary result. So that, upon the whole, I think I may safely boast of being descended from valiant ancestors. . . .

My ancestors lived in retirement in the valley of Ambra, where they were lords of considerable domains; they were all trained to arms, and distinguished for military prowess. One of the family, a youth named Cristofano, had a fierce dispute with some of their neighbors and friends; and because the chief relations on both sides had engaged in the dispute, and it seemed likely that the flames of discord would end in the destruction of the two families, the eldest people, having maturely considered the matter, unanimously agreed to remove the two young men who began the quarrel out of the way. The opposite party obliged their kinsman to withdraw to Siena, and Cristofano's parents sent him to Florence, where they purchased a small house for him in the Via Chiara, from the monastery of St. Ursula, with a pretty good estate near the bridge of Rofredi. This Cristofano married in Florence, and had several sons and daughters: the daughters were portioned off; and the sons divided the remainder of their father's substance between them. After his decease, the house of Via Chiara, with some other property of no great amount, fell to one of the above-mentioned sons, whose name was Andrea. He took a wife, by whom he had four male children: the name of the first was Girolamo, that of the second Bartolomeo; the third was Giovanni, my father; the fourth was Francesco.

Andrea Cellini, my grandfather, was tolerably well versed in the architecture of those days, and made it his profession. Giovanni, my father, cultivated it more than any of his brothers; and since, according to the opinion of Vitruvius, those who are desirous of succeeding in this art, should, amongst other things, know something of music and drawing, Giovanni, having acquired great proficiency in the art of designing, began to apply himself to music. He learned to play admirably well upon the viol and flute; and being of a very studious disposition, he hardly ever went abroad.

His next-door neighbor was Stefano Granacci, who had several daughters of extraordinary beauty. Giovanni soon became sensible to the charms of one of them, named Lisabetta; and at length grew so deeply enamoured that he asked her in marriage. Their fathers being intimate, and next-door neighbors, it was no difficult matter to bring about the match, as both parties thought they found their account in it. First of all, the two old men concluded the marriage, and then began to talk of the portion; but they could not rightly agree on that point, for Andrea said to Stefano, "My son Giovanni is the best youth in Florence, and even in all Italy; and if I had thought of procuring him a wife before, I might have obtained for him the best portion in Florence amongst persons of our rank." Stefano answered, "You have a thousand reasons on your side, but I have five daughters and several sons; so that, all things duly considered, it is as much as I can afford." Giovanni had stood some time listening to their conversation unperceived by them, but on hearing this he suddenly interrupted them, saying, "Ah! father, it is the girl that I love and desire, and not her money. Wretched is he who married to repair his fortune by means of his wife's dowry. You boast that I am possessed of some talents; is it then to be supposed that I am unable to maintain my wife, and supply her necessities? I want nothing of you but your consent; and I must give you to understand that the girl shall be mine; as to the portion, you may take it yourself." Andrea Cellini, who was somewhat eccentric, was not a little displeased at this; but in a few days Giovanni took his wife home, and never afterwards required any portion of her father.

They enjoyed their consecrated love for eighteen years; but had no children, which they ardently desired. At the expiration of the eighteenth year, however, Giovanni's wife miscarried of two male children, through the unskilfulness of her medical attendants. She became pregnant again, and gave birth to a girl, who was called Rosa, after my father's mother. Two years after, she was once more with child, and, as women in her condition are liable to certain longings, hers being exactly the same upon this occasion as before, it was generally thought that she would have another girl, and it had been already agreed to give her the name of Reparata, after my mother's mother. It happened that she was brought to bed precisely the night of All-Saints-day, in the year 1500, at half an hour past four. The midwife, who was sensible that the family expected the birth of a female, as soon as she had washed the child and wrapped it up in fine swaddling clothes, came softly up to my father, and said to him, "I here bring you a fine present which you little expected." My father, who was of a philosophical disposition, and happened to be then walking about, said, "What God gives me, I shall always receive thankfully;" but, taking off the clothes, he saw with his own eyes the unexpected boy. Clasping his hands together, he lifted up his eyes to Heaven, saying: "Lord, I thank thee from the bottom of my heart for this present, which is very dear and welcome to me." The standers-by asked him, joyfully, how he proposed to call the child: he made them no other answer than, "He is WELCOME." And this name of Welcome (VENVENUTO) he resolved to give me at the font; and so I was christened accordingly.

BENVENUTO CELLINI
Autobiography, 1588

In making the Grand Tour of Napolenoic Europe in the first decade of the nineteenth century, young George Gordon, Lord Byron, was doing no more than other Englishmen of his station did by way of finishing off their schooling. But by transforming that experience into Childe Harold's Pilgrimage *he was doing more than any predecessor ever had. Byron's verse travelog, which sated his society's craving for romantic travel literature, created a sensation: in the poet's oft-repeated assessment, "I woke up one morning and found myself famous." To satisfy his readers' demands, Byron expanded his tale of the wandering nobleman, the "Childe" of the poem's title, from two cantos to three and eventually to four. With the fourth canto, from which the following lines are taken, Byron drops the device of the narrator-hero to speak directly to the reader about the great cities of Italy.*

A HUNDRED TALES OF LOVE

Yet, Italy, through every other land
Thy wrongs should ring, and shall, from side to side!
Mother of Arts, as once of arms, thy hand
Was then our guardian, and is still our guide!
Parent of our Religion, whom the wide
Nations have knelt to for the keys of heaven!

Europe, repentant of her parricide,
Shall yet redeem thee, and, all backward driven,
Roll the barbarian tide, and sue to be forgiven.

But Arno wins us to the fair white walls
Where the Etrurian Athens claims and keeps
A softer feeling for her fairy halls.
Girt by her theatre of hills, she reaps
Her corn and wine and oil, and Plenty leaps
To laughing life with her redundant horn.
Along the banks where smiling Arno sweeps
Was modern Luxury of Commerce born,
And buried Learning rose, redeemed to a new morn.

There, too, the Goddess loves in stone, and fills
The air around with beauty; we inhale
The ambrosial aspect, which beheld instils
Part of its immortality; the veil
Of heaven is half undrawn; within the pale
We stand, and in that form and face behold
What Mind can make when Nature's self would fail,
And to the fond idolators of old
Envy the innate flash which such a soul could mould.

We gaze and turn away, and know not where,
Dazzled and drunk with beauty, till the hart
Reels with its fulness; there—for ever there—
Chained to the chariot of triumphal Art,
We stand as captives, and would not depart.
Away!—there need no words, nor terms precise,
The paltry jargon of the marble mart,
Where Pedantry gulls Folly—we have eyes:
Blood, pulse, and breast confirm the Dardan Shepherd's prize.

Appearedst thou not to Paris in this guise,
Or to more deeply blest Anchises? or,
In all thy perfect goddess-ship, when lies
Before thee thy own vanquished Lord of War,
And gazing in thy face as toward a star,
Laid on thy lap, his eyes to thee upturn,
Feeding on thy sweet cheek, while thy lips are
With lava kisses melting while they burn,
Showered on his eyelids, brow, and mouth, as from an urn?

Glowing, and circumfused in speechless love,
Their full divinity and inadequate
That feeling to express or to improve,
The gods become as mortals, and man's fate
Has moments like their brightest; but the weight
Of earth recoils upon us;—let it go!
We can recall such visions, and create,

From what has been or might be, things which grow
Into thy statue's form and look like gods below.

I leave to learned fingers and wise hands,
The artist and his ape, to teach and tell
How well his connoisseurship understands
The graceful bend and the voluptuous swell:
Let these describe the undescribable;
I would not their vile breath should crisp the stream
Wherein that image shall for ever dwell,
The unruffled mirror of the loveliest dream
That ever left the sky on the deep soul to beam.

In Santa Croce's holy precincts lie
Ashes which make it holier, dust which is
Even in itself an immortality,
Though there were nothing save the past, and this,
The particle of those sublimities
Which have relapsed to chaos; here repose
Angelo's, Alfieri's bones, and his,
The starry Galileo, with his woes;
Here Machiavelli's earth returned to whence it rose.

These are four minds, which, like the elements,
Might furnish forth creation.—Italy!
Time, which hath wronged thee with ten thousand rents
Of thine imperial garment, shall deny,
And hath denied, to every other sky,
Spirits which soar from ruin: thy decay
Is still imprenate with divinity,
Which gilds it with revivifying ray;
Such as the great of yore Canova is to-day.

But where repose the all-Etruscan three—
Dante, and Petrarch, and, scarce less than they,
The Bard of Prose, creative spirit, he
Of the Hunded Tales of love—where did they lay
Their bones, distinguished from our common clay
In death as life? Are they resolved to dust,
And have their country's marbles nought to say?
Could not her quarries furnish forth one bust?
Did they not to her breast their filial earth entrust?

Ungrateful Florence! Dante sleeps afar,
Like Scipio, buried by the upbraiding shore:
Thy factions, in their worse than civil war,
Proscribed the bard whose name for everymore
Their children's children would in vain adore
With the remorse of ages; and the crown
Which Petrarch's laureate brow supremely wore,
Upon a far and foreign soil had grown,
His life, his fame, his grave, though rifled—not thine own

Boccaccio to his parent earth bequeathed
His dust,—and lies it not her great among,
With many a sweet and solemn requiem breathed
O'er him who formed the Tuscan's siren tongue,
That music in itself, whose sounds are song,
The poetry of speech? No; even his tomb
Uptorn must bear the hyaena bigot's wrong,
No more amidst the meaner dead find room,
Nor claim a passing sigh, because it told for *whom*!

And Santa Croce wants their mighty dust;
Yet for this want more noted, as of yore
The Caesar's pageant, shorn of Brutus' bust,
Did but of Rome's best son remind her more:
Happier Ravenna! on thy hoary shore,
Fortress of falling empire, honored sleeps
The immortal exile,—Arqua, too, her store
Of tuneful relics proudly claims and keeps,
While Florence vainly begs her banished dead and weeps.

What is her pyramid of precious stones,
Of porphyry, jasper, agage, and all hues
Of gem and marble, to encrust the bones
Of merchant-dukes? the momentary dews
Which, sparkling to the twilight stars, infuse
Freshness in the green turf that wraps the dead
Whose names are mausoleums of the Muse,
Are gently pressed with far more reverent tread
Than ever paced the slab which paves the princely head.

LORD BYRON
Childe Harold's Pilgrimage, 1818

There have been more passionate love affairs than that of the poets Robert Browning and Elizabeth Barrett, but there is no more passionate love-correspondence in all of literature than theirs. It sustained them during their clandestine courtship, when Miss Barrett's despotic father sought to prevent her from seeing the younger poet, and it continued after they eloped to Pisa and ultimately settled in Florence. There, despite the distractions of attending to his invalid wife, Robert Browning was to produce several important poetic cycles, among them the one from which "The Statue and the Bust," excerpted below, is taken.

There's a palace in Florence, the world knows well,
And a statue watches it from the square,
And this story of both do our townsmen tell.

Ages ago, a lady there,
At the farthest window facing the East
Asked, 'Who rides by with the royal air?'

The brides-maids' prattle around her ceased;
She leaned forth, one on either hand;
They saw how the blush of the bride increased—

They felt by its beat her heart expand—
As one at each ear and both in a breath
Whispered, 'The Great-Duke Ferdinand.'

That selfsame instant, underneath,
The Duke rode past in his idle way,
Empty and fine like a swordless sheath.

Gay he rode, with a friend as gay,
Till he threw his head back—'Who is she?'
—'A Bride the Riccardi brings home to-day.'

Hair in heaps lay heavily
Over a pale brow spirit-pure—
Carved like the heart of the coal-black tree,

Crisped like a war-steed's encolure—
And vainly sought to dissemble her eyes
Of the blackest black our eyes endure.

And lo, a blade for a knight's emprise
Filled the fine empty sheath of a man,—
The Duke grew straightway brave and wise.

He looked at her, as a lover can;
She looked at him, as one who awakes,—
The Past was a sleep, and her life began.

Now, love so ordered for both their sakes,
A feast was held that selfsame night
In the pile which the mighty shadow makes.

(For Via Larga is three-parts light,
But the Palace overshadows one,
Because of a crime which may God require!

To Florence and God the wrong was done,
Through the first republic's murder there
By Cosimo and his cursed son.)

The Duke (with the statue's face in the square)
Turned in the midst of his multitude
At the bright approach of the bridal pair.

Face to face the lovers stood
A single minute and no more,
While the bridegroom bent as a man subdued—

Bowed till his bonnet brushed the floor—
For the Duke on the lady a kiss conferred,
As the courtly custom was of yore.

In a minute can lovers exchange a word?
If a word did pass, which I do not think,
Only one out of the thousand heard.

ROBERT BROWNING
"*The Statue and the Bust,*" 1850

AIDED BY
GOD'S GRACE

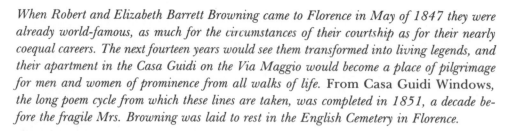

When Robert and Elizabeth Barrett Browning came to Florence in May of 1847 they were already world-famous, as much for the circumstances of their courtship as for their nearly coequal careers. The next fourteen years would see them transformed into living legends, and their apartment in the Casa Guidi on the Via Maggio would become a place of pilgrimage for men and women of prominence from all walks of life. From Casa Guidi Windows, the long poem cycle from which these lines are taken, was completed in 1851, a decade before the fragile Mrs. Browning was laid to rest in the English Cemetery in Florence.

The day was such a day
  As Florence owes the sun. The sky above,
Its weight upon the mountains seemed to lay,
  And palpitate in glory, like a dove
Who has flown too fast, full-hearted—take away
  The image! for the heart of man beat higher
That day in Florence, flooding all her streets
  And piazzas with a tumult and desire.
The people, with accumulated heats
  ·And faces turned one way, as if one fire
Both drew and flushed them, left their ancient beats
  And went up towards the palace Pitti wall
To thank their Grand-duke who, not quite of course,
  Had graciously permitted, at their call,
The citizens to use their civic force
  To guard their civic homes. So, one and all,
The Tuscan cities streamed up to the source
  Of this new good at Florence, taking it
As good so far, presageful of more good,—
  The first torch of Italian freedom, lit
To toss in the next tiger's face who should
  Approach too near them in a greedy fit,—
The first pulse of an even flow of blood
  To prove the level of Italian veins
Towards rights perceived and granted. How we gazed
  From Casa Guidi windows while, in trains
Of orderly procession—banners raised,
  And intermittent bursts of marital strains
Which died upon the shouts, as if amazed
  By gladness beyond music—they passed on!
The Magistracy, with insignia, passed,—
  And all the people shouted in the sun,
And all the thousand windows which had cast
  A ripple of silks in blue and scarlet down
(As if the houses overflowed at last),
  Seemed growing larger with fair heads and eyes.
The Lawyers passed,—and still arose the shout,
  And hands broke from the windows to surprise
Those grave calm brows with bay-tree leaves thrown out.
  The Priesthood passed,—the friars with worldly-wise
Keen sidelong glances from their beards about
  The street to see who shouted; many a monk
Who takes a long rope in the waist, was there:

Whereat the popular exultation drunk
With indrawn 'vivas' the whole sunny air,
   While through the murmuring windows rose and sunk
A cloud of kerchiefed hands,—'The church makes fair
   Her welcome in the new Pope's name.'' Ensued
The black sign of the 'Martyrs'—(name no name,
   But count the graves in silence). Next were viewed
The Artists; next, the Trades; and after came
   The People,—flag and sign, and rights as good—
And very loud the shout was for that same
   Motto, 'Il popolo.' IL POPOLO,—
The word means dukedom, empire, majesty,
   And kings in such an hour might read it so.
And next, with banners, each in his degree,
   Deputed representatives a-row
Of every separate state of Tuscany:
   Siena's she-wolf, bristling on the fold
Of the first flag, preceded Pisa's hare,
   And Massa's long floated calm in gold,
Pienza's following with his silver stare.
   Arezzo's steed pranced clear from bridle-hold,—
And well might shout our Florence, greeting there
   These, and more brethren. Last, the world had sent
The various children of her teeming flanks—
   Greeks, English, French—as if to a parliament
Of lovers of her Italy in ranks,
   Each bearing its land's symbol reverent;
At which the stones seemed breaking into thanks
   And rattling up the sky, such sounds in proof
Arose; the very house-walls seemed to bend;
   The very windows, up from door to roof,
Flashed out a rapture of bright heads, to mend
   With passionate looks the gesture's whirling off
A hurricane of leaves. Three hours did end
   While all these passed; and ever in the crowd,
Rude men, unconscious of the tears that kept
   Their beards moist, shouted; some few laughed aloud.
And none asked any why they laughed and wept:
   Friends kissed each other's cheeks, and foes long vowed
More warmly did it; two months' babies leapt
   Right upward in their mother's arms, whose black
Wide glittering eyes looked elsewhere; lovers pressed
   Each before either, neither glancing back;
And peasant maidens smoothly 'tired and tressed
   Forgot to finger on their throats the slack
Great pearl-strings; while old blind men would not rest,
   But pattered with their staves and slid their shoes
Along the stones, and smiled as if they saw.
   O heaven, I think that day had noble use
Among God's days! So near stood Right and Law,
   Both mutually forborne! Law would not bruise

Nor Right deny, and each in reverent awe
   Honored the other. And if, ne'ertheless,
That good day's sun delivered to the vines
   No charta, and the liberal Duke's excess
Did scarce exceed a Guelf's or Ghibelline's
   In any special actual righteousness
Of what that day he granted, still the signs
   Are good and full of promise, we must say,
When multitudes approach their kings with prayers
   And kings concede their people's right to pray
Both in one sunshine. Griefs are not despairs,
   So uttered, nor can royal claims dismay
When men from humble homes and ducal chairs
   Hate wrong together. It was well to view
Those banners ruffled in a ruler's face
   Inscribed, 'Live freedom, union, and all true
Brave patriots who are aided by God's grace!'
   Nor was it ill when Leopoldo drew
His little children to the window-place
   He stood in at the Pitti, to suggest
They too should govern as the people willed.
   What a cry rose then! some, who saw the best,
Declared his eyes filled up and overfilled
   With good warm human tears which unrepressed
Ran down. I like his face; the forehead's build
   Has no capacious genius, yet perhaps
Sufficient comprehension,—mild and sad,
   And careful nobly,—not with care that wraps
Self-loving hearts, to stifle and make mad,
   But careful with the care that shuns a lapse
Of faith and duty, studious not to add
   A burden in the gathering of a gain.
And so, God save the Duke, I say with those
   Who that day shouted it; and while dukes reign,
May all wear in the visible overflows
   Of spirit, such a look of careful pain!
For God must love it better than respose.

ELIZABETH BARRETT BROWNING
From Casa Guidi Windows, 1851

Hippolyte Taine, a writer not known for his effusiveness, greeted Jacob Burckhardt's Civilization of the Renaissance in Italy *as "an admirable book, the most complete and philosophical one that has been written on the Italian Renaissance." Admirable indeed: Burckhardt's monumental work was to spark a new enthusiasm for the epoch and a new approach to history as well. In the words of Hajo Holborn, writing exactly one century after the first publication of* Civilization: *"In Burckhardt's hands the conception of an age of the Renaissance received a new context, a novel application and valid historical meaning. He explained the growth of the new individualism by the political and social developments of Italy in the later Middle Ages, while the rebirth of classical learning was an invigorating, but only subsidiary, element in the evolution of the new philosophy of life."*

The most elevated political thought and the most varied forms of human development are found united in the history of Florence, which in this sense deserves the name of the first modern State in the world. Here the whole people are busied with what in the despotic cities is the affair of a single family. That wondrous Florentine spirit, at once keenly critical and artistically creative, was incessantly transforming the social and political condition of the State, and as incessantly describing and judging the change. Florence thus became the home of political doctrines and theories, of experiments and sudden changes, but also, like Venice, the home of statistical science, and alone and above all other States in the world, the home of historical representation in the modern sense of the phrase. The spectacle of ancient Rome and a familiarity with its leading writers were not without influence; Giovanni Villani confesses that he received the first impulse to his great work at the jubilee of the year 1300, and began it immediately on his return home. Yet how many among the 200,000 pilgrims of that year may have been like him in gifts and tendencies and still did not write the history of their native cities! For not all of them could encourage themselves with the thought: 'Rome is sinking; my native city is rising, and ready to achieve great things, and therefore I wish to relate its past history, and hope to continue the story to the present time, and as long as my life shall last.' And besides the witness to its past, Florence obtained through its historians . . . a greater fame than fell to the lot of any other city in Italy. . . .

Florence not only existed under political forms more varied than those of the free States of Italy and of Europe generally, but it reflected upon them far more deeply. It is a faithful mirror of the relations of individuals and classes to a variable whole. The pictures of the great civic democracies in France and in Flanders, as they are delineated in Froissart, and the narratives of the German chroniclers of the fourteenth century, are in truth of high importance; but in comprehensiveness of thought and in the rational development of the story, none will bear comparison with the Florentines. The rule of the nobility, the tyrannies, the struggles of the middle class with the proletariat, limited and unlimited democracy, pseudo-democracy, the primacy or a single house, the theocracy of Savonarola, and the mixed forms of government which prepared the way for the Medicean despotism—all are so described that the inmost motives of the actors are laid bare to the light. At length Machiavelli in his Florentine history (down to 1492) represents his native city as a living organism and its development as a natural and individual process; he is the first of the moderns who has risen to such a conception. It lies without our province to determine whether and in what points Machiavelli may have done violence to history, as is notoriously the case in his life of Castruccio Castracani—a fancy picture of the typical despot. We might find something to say against every line of the "Storie Fiorentine," and yet the great and unique value of the whole would remain unaffected. And his contemporaries and successors, Jacopo Pitti, Guicciardini Segni, Varchi, Vettori, what a circle of illustrious names! And what a story it is which these masters tell us! The great and memorable drama of the last decades of the Florentine republic is here unfolded. The voluminous record of the collapse of the highest and most original life which the world could then show may appear to

one but as a collection of curiosities, may awaken in another a devilish delight at the shipwreck of so much nobility and grandeur, to a third may seem like a great historical assize; for all it will be an object of thought and study to the end of time. The evil which was for ever troubling the peace of the city was its rule over once powerful and now conquered rivals like Pisa—a rule of which the necessary consequence was a chronic state of violence. The only remedy, certainly an extreme one and which none but Savonarola could have persuaded Florence to accept, and that only with the help of favorable chances, would have been the well-timed dissolution of Tuscany into a federal union of free cities. At a later period this scheme, then no more than the dream of a past age, brought (1548) a patriotic citizen of Lucca to the scaffold. From this evil and from the ill-starred Guelph sympathies of Florence for a foreign prince, which familiarized it with foreign intervention, came all the disasters which followed. But who does not admire the people which was wrought up by its venerated preacher to a mood of such sustained loftiness that for the first time in Italy it set the example of sparing a conquered foe, while the whole history of its past taught nothing but vengeance and extermination? The glow which melted patriotism into one with moral regeneration may seem, when looked at from a distance, to have soon passed away; but its best results shine forth again in the memorable siege of 1529-30. They were "fools," as Guicciardini then wrote, who drew down this storm upon Florence, but he confesses himself that they achieved things which seemed incredible; and when he declares that sensible people would have got out of the way of the danger, he means no more than that Florence ought to have yielded itself silently and ingloriously into the hands of its enemies. It would no doubt have preserved its splendid suburbs and gardens, and the lives and prosperity of countless citizens; but it would have been the poorer by one of its greatest and most ennobling memories.

In many of their chief merits the Florentines are the pattern and the earliest type of Italians and modern Europeans generally; they are so also in many of their defects. When Dante compares the city which was always mending its constitution with the sick man who is continually changing his posture to escape from pain, he touches with the comparison a permanent feature of the political life of Florence. The great modern fallacy that a constitution can be made, can be manufactured by a combination of existing forces and tendencies, was constantly cropping up in stormy times; even Machiavelli is not wholly free from it. Constitutional artists were never wanting who by an ingenious distribution and division of political power, by indirect elections of the most complicated kind, by the establishment of nominal offices, sought to found a lasting order of things, and to satisfy or to deceive the rich and the poor alike. They naively fetch their examples from classical antiquity, and borrow the party names "ottimati," "aristocrazia," as a matter of course. The world since then has become used to these expressions and given them a conventional European sense, whereas all former party names were purely national, and either characterized the cause at issue or sprang from the caprice of accident.

JACOB BURCKHARDT
Civilization of the Renaissance in Italy, 1860

"Desolazione" Katherine Kressman Taylor calls the final section of her Diary of Florence in Flood, *and indeed desolation is the only word to describe the impact of the disastrous flood of 1966 on the birthplace of the Renaissance. Not since 1333 had the dark, roiling waters of the Arno risen so high, and never had they done such damage. Worse than the damage done to the city by occupying Nazi troops in World War II, this invasion of water-carried muck and silt was to carry off the marble revetments of the Duomo, panels from the great doors of the Baptistry, and statues from the Arno bridges. All this desolation was witnessed by novelist Taylor, beginning on a fateful fiesta day in November, 1966.*

The festa celebrating Italian victory in the First World War falls on November 4, and in Florence the rain-coated crowds pouring homeward through the narrow streets in the center of town at six on the evening of the third look cheerful in spite of the downpour. *Domani è festa*, the shops will be closed, there will be a holiday from work. . . .

This is, however, a torrential rain. October was a wet month all through Northern Italy, and after two bright days November has settled down to outdo October with a new drenching. Women protected by umbrellas and overshoes shrink into doorways to wait for a respite in the driving rain that will soak them to the knees within fifty feet, but there is no letup. Buses pass, crammed to the doors, all the taxis filled already. Impatient young men cover their heads with copies of the *Nazione Sera*, wrap their overcoats tightly around them, and set off through the deluge.

Sloshing homeward, my umbrella twisting under the wet wind (I have just been for a fitting of a winter skirt in Via Porta Santa Maria near the Ponte Vecchio), I catch a jammed bus for a few blocks to the Ponte Amerigo Vespucci and then hug the palace fronts along the lungarno, to arrive, *tutta bagnata*, at the huge wooden outer doors of the *pensione* on the Arno. It is a night to stay indoors, despite a concert in the Hall of the Five Hundred, a night for a hot bath and a cognac, bed and a good book, with the sound of the rain drumming on the shutters. . . .

Dawn comes at six with a faint gleam of gray through the slats of the shutters (all Italian houses are sealed tight during the night), but a flick of the switch of the bedside lamp brings no responsive glow of light. A cigarette lighter shows the hour. I stumble out of bed and grope my way to the wall switch, which proves dead too, and then feel my way through the gloom of the windows and push the shutters back into their recesses. My first impression is that it is darkly overcast and still raining hard; then I stand gaping at the river. . . .

A tumultuous mass of water stretches from bank to bank, perhaps four feet below the tops of the twenty-five-foot walls, a snarling brown torrent of terrific velocity, spiraling in whirlpools and countercurrents that send waves running backward; and its color is a rich brown, a boiling *caffè-latte* brown streaked with crests the color of dirty cream. This tremendous water carries mats of debris: straw, twigs, leafy branches, rags, a littler that the river sucks down and spews up again in a swelling turbulence. Its thunderous rush holds me tense at the window, as any movement of great force can lay a spell on the eyes. All I can think of is that it is as magnificent as it is threatening, a river in spate moving at full stress, its surface twisting with curling ropes of water that smack together and go up in spouts of foam. The flood is absolute as a forest fire is absolute or a full gale stripping the country-side and bending down all the trees.

Here down the torrent comes a tree, uprooted, the tangled root structure washed clean by the water, the branches trailing thick leaves. A red oil drum comes bobbing high; then two more trees slide by, their roots a floating snarl—and how bit they are! There must have been terrible cloudbursts up in the hills of the Casentino when we had that drenching rain last night—this same drenching rain, for it is still coming down in *scrosci*. There are electric lights visible in two buildings across the Arno, but these go out while I am watching, while the dawn-light is still closer to darkness than to day.

I mark a measuring point on the opposite side, a hole in the brick front of the rock-crushing plant, whose flat-bottomed barges are leaping and clashing together at their moorings, and after a few minutes' watch I conclude that the river is still rising. It can't be far below the wall that protects the Lugarno on this side, and this stretch of street is a high point on the waterfront. Looking upstream toward the Ponte Vespucci I hazard a guess that the water is about two feet below the span of the arch. There will be real damage done if the Arno should bring all this pressure against the bridges themselves. I wonder about the Ponte Vecchio upriver at the center of town, for the ancient bridge built by Taddeo Gaddi in 1345 is not strong and is very low; there was concern for that old landmark some years ago in the high water of November. . . .

The lobby is gray and tranquil, and everything seems normal and everyday: the Signora is standing looking calmly out the great arched doorway toward the river, and Aldo, the curly-haired young *cameriere*, is mopping the marble floor, preparing for the day and the descent of the guests. The wide staircase with its marble balustrade and red velvet carpet curves up into the gloom, and there is no sound of movement in the little palace. I feel a strong sense of emergency, none the less. The Signora smiles at my concern. There has not been a flood in Florence since the eighteen forties, and that one, like every year's high water, spilled out over the lowlands down river from the town.

"*L'Arno sempre contiene la piena*," she assures me with confidence. It is the season of autumn rains, and the Arno must be expected to run full. She explains that there are dams upstream and that now some of the dam gates will have been opened to protect the upper reaches, but the high water is simply running through here to spill itself in the sea below Pisa. Her assurance, as I shall learn later, is common among Florentines, who have never in living memory known the Arno as a threat and are completely and tragically unprepared to deal with one when it comes. Outside, the rain falls with no sign of moderating. . . .

There are few persons in the street. Some look excited; those coming toward us from the center look dazed. At the second bridge, Ponte alla Carraia, we come to a standstill, for looking east from the platform there, the short distance down toward Ponte Vecchio, we can see deep water in the street and, after a second unbelieving look, water pouring over the walls between the old bridge and beautiful Ponte Santa Trinita. The river is in the town. . . .

A number of cars are still crossing the high Ponte della Vittoria downstream from us and on our level, but toward the heart of town Ponte Amerigo Vespucci, Ponte alla Carraia, and Ponte Santa Trinitia are closed to wheeled traffic. Around their piers our once-gentle Arno is raging like a sea in storm. A few human figures are hurrying across the bridges on foot. On Ponte Vespucci four raincoated figures appear, trotting toward the other side of Arno in a line, holding umbrellas before them at an identical cant. In their dark clothes they are picked out in the murk like people in a Japanese painting—the four black silhouettes bent forward, the black umbrellas, the brown water, the rain.

No arch shows any longer beneath Ponte Vespucci, the tide is leaning against the bridge itself, and the great tree trunks riding down strike thunderously against the cement, throwing up a twenty-foot wash of water and a high cloud of spray that slowly drifts away. The water level crawls even higher. . . .

Some of us who have transistors have heard a broadcast or two: the Santa Croce area is swamped, there is a meter and a half of water in the Piazza del Duomo, but as yet no houses have crumbled and no reports of deaths have come in. Our adventurous young friend who ran down clear past the borders of the flooded area reports a meter of water in the streets at Ponte Santa Trinita, and he keeps trying to make us understand how fast the water is running: nobody could stand against it, cars are being swept along and overturned. He wants us to take a look at the river out there and try to realize how furiously the water is moving. . . .

We go back to our vigil at the windows of the *salotto*, realizing all too well that the emergency is growing worse, feeling sick with the knowledge of what must be happening to this elegant and beloved city, but with no concern in proportion to what is actually in store for her. . . . The color of the river has thickened to a dark, ugly brown, and the water is streaked with black and yellow oil, an incredible amount of oil like a crud on the tempestuous surface. It isn't bringing calm to these troubled waters, whatever this oil is, wherever it can be coming from, wherever all these tons of water can be coming from.

One of the men puts on his raincoat again and runs down the staircase and across the street; he leans over the wall, thrusts down an arm, and brings it up with his hand dripping. A foot down, maybe. . . .

By 3:30 the flood is lapping the top of the wall, and spouts of water like a dozen garden hoses spurt through apertures that are beginning to appear between the bricks. The flood is obviously reaching for us, and a few of us start putting on boots and raincoats for a last sortie, not as gawkers this time but from the pressing need to see with our own eyes the actual extent of the peril. If a venture is to be made, it must be made now, for the wall is obviously threatened and the day is growing dark. "*Come fa buio a quest' ora*," mutters Albarosa at her desk in the lower hall, where she has lighted a stubby candle against the growing gloom. . . .

The rain has thinned to a drizzle. Past the piazza a block away, the Lungarno is covered by a three-inch layer of water; within the next two squares it becomes a mush of muddy water (with unexpected potholes), which splashes over the tops of galoshes every dozen steps. A helicopter goes over, flying low along the river, and somebody identifies it as belonging to the *Paris Match*, whose daredevil photographers will take any risk to get pictures, the first sign we have had that the outside world knows about Florence and her plight. . . .

In the square itself the broad cascade from the street explodes in a vortex of waves, whirlpools, and debris—branches, an oil drum, which it

smashes against a wall, then against a shopfront—carrying too a float of twigs, shoes, pocketbooks, and paper, which swing round and round in a crazy bobbing dance. A strong current sweeps the car toward the shops—these sealed with great steel shutters because the day is a holiday—and slams it headfirst against a shutter, which shivers and begins to bulge under the battering. All the shops are taking a battering from the debris and from the heavily swirling water, and as we gaze in a sort of stupor we see that the two art galleries at the center of the square are going to go, and very shortly; nothing can continue to take this for long. We turn our eyes away; we don't want to see it.

In endless onrush the waters pile in, the swamped square finding its outlet along the famous Borgo Ognissanti. It is almost a straight sweep through from the flood pouring into the square and Ognissanti itself, now become a river racing onward toward the Prato, its entrance partially blocked by a jumble of upturned cars and leafy branches that makes the flood boil as it tears its way through and past. This flood in Ognissanti, now three feet deep and wall to wall, will race with nine to twelve feet of water before three hours are up, to continue to drum and roar at this damaging pace for eight or nine hours longer at full height. . . .

Heartsick, our uneasiness tinged with dread, we turn back along the Lugarno, sloshing through deepening water in the street, through which a strong current is beginning to run, so that we hasten our steps, pushing our way along, boots full and feet icy. There is much water spouting through the weak spots in the retaining wall. Beyond the wall, the river is coming down against the Ponte Vespucci like an avalanche, butting against the superstructure and shaking it and then boiling back in a great rumpus of waves, which come on again harder than before. One of the iron railings has been cracked and wrenched askew.

Before we reach the high point where our little palace-*pensione* stands, the dirty tide is already beginning to creep along the street out front, and we join Dario, who stands impatiently at the huge wooden outer doors, waiting for the last foolish venturer to get back to safety. We watch him appear through the mist of the rain, a dignified elderly gentleman who was once an American consul general in Italy and who is fond of these people and feels a responsibility toward them. He goes in ankle deep between midstreet and sidewalk and comes slowly into the entry, shaking his head. In the open doorway our little Signora stands with her arms clutched against her waist, wailing softly, "*Quest'Arno, quest'Arno!*" as if reproving a delinquent child.

The great front doors are locked and the heavy bolt shot home, and Dario carries down an armload of sacks. The boys are removing the red velvet carpet from the stairs that go down into the entryway. Out back the courtyard is filling with water despite our brave little dike. . . .

Between our house and Ponte della Vittoria—downstream, cutting us off as if on an island—suddenly we see the river sweeping straight in over the top of the wall. . . .

Already the water is coming in under the great front doors of the entryway three feet below the level of the floor of the downstairs hall, and guests and servants begin carrying mattresses and furniture up the wide, velvet-carpeted staircase. In half an hour the upstairs hall is piled full with these refugee pieces and with the suitcases and overcoats of the ground-floor guests. Our venturesome young man has inanely left two pairs of sodden oxfords on top of a cold radiator. The professor reports that in the courtyard out back the water is up to the fenders of the cars, but there is curiously little oil out there; the water has been seeping under our little dike and has not yet started to run over it. . . .

The Italian news broadcast comes on at five. The chatterers are shushed, and the three of us who understand something of the language strain our ears to catch what we can from the rapid Italian voices on the air. We learn that Florence is isolated. All Tuscany is suffering from floods, and we are cut off by rail and road and telephone from Rome to the south and Bologna to the north. The heavy storm is general all over Italy; high winds have done damage in Sicily, in Naples, with huge trees uprooted on Capri. No help can reach Florence in this catastrophe. . . .

At ten o'clock there is another news broadcast: Florence is a lake—an absurdly placid metaphore, this! There are three meters of water—that means ten feet!—in the Piazza del Duomo, and isolated families are calling for help from second-floor windows. All afternoon army helicopters from the parachutist brigade at Livorno have been rescuing people stranded on rooftops in the lowest sections of the city; only women and children have been taken; the men have been left on the roofs to wait for succor on another day. So that is what those helicopters were doing! Pisa is flooded. Pisa, which lies at the mouth of the Arno and is receiving the whole flow of the river, has sent Florence a message begging for help and has been refused. Florence cannot help herself. . . .

Some time between eleven and midnight a candle appears in the doorway of the *salotto* and above it Dario's face alight with good tidings. "*Scende,*" he calls out excitedly. "*L'acqua scende!*" The water is going down. We cannot believe it. We all pile down the stairs with our candles in our hands, and incredibly there is the wet and the oil mark on the wall of the entry showing where the flood reached and on the highest riser bare inches from the floor, but the pool within the doors has shrunk, the water is down almost to the second step. . . .

But even yet we are a little reluctant to trust the behavior of the river. The line that shows where the water came to is daubed on the entry walls—not two inches from the floor. Dario and the Signora tell us with determination that we shall sleep more restfully in our own beds than on mattresses laid out dormitory style in the *salotto*. The luggage is left heaped where we dumped it earlier, but mattresses and blankets go down the stairs, and the boys put our comfortable beds together. Dario will be our guarantee and will stand guard all night, and though we protest a little, we are glad enough to have him out there on watch as we snuff out our candle stubs and stumble between the sheets, feeling physically exhausted and emotionally spent. We sleep with shutters open, for no servant has thought to close them on this floor according to the peaceful routine of the house; and, alas, what intruder is there to fear; who could approach through that millrace out there in the street, along the overflowing river? In total blackness, heads sunk in our pillows, matches close at hand in case of emergency, we listen through waves of drowsiness to the roar of the Arno.

KATHERINE KRESSMAN TAYLOR
Diary of Florence in Flood, 1967

REFERENCE

Chronology of Florentine History

c. 200 B.C.	Etruscans establish colony on banks of the Arno below Fiesole on future site of Florence
83	Lucius Cornelius Sulla conquers Etruscans and occupies their settlement on the Arno
A.D. 250	Martyrdom of Minias (later San Miniato)
393	San Lorenzo consecrated by Saint Ambrose, bishop of Milan; serves for some time as the growing city's first cathedral
405	Florence besieged by Ostrogoths
476	Romulus Augustus, last Emperor of the West, abdicates his throne
541	Florence "liberated" from Goths by Byzantine troops, who establish headquarters in the last Roman buildings in town—the baths, theatre, and capitol in central part of the city
565	Death of Justinian, last Emperor of the West; Dark Ages ensue, during which Florence is gradually depopulated
570	Lombards conquer Florence
774	Charlemagne subdues the Lombards and takes possession of all Tuscany, including Florence; on three visits to the city he founds churches
825	Emperor Lothair establishes one of Italy's eight ecclesiastical schools in Florence
1013	Monastery of San Miniato founded
1073	Death of Gualberti, founder of the Vallombrosan order of monks
1107	Florentines, growing in military strength, destroy castle at Monte Cascioli, attack Prato
1125	Fiesole brought under siege by Florentines
1208	Otto of Saxony assumes control of Tuscany
1211	First Franciscan settlement in Florence
1215	Assassination of Buondelmonte dei Buondelmonti sparks Guelph-Ghibelline feud
1218	Ponte alla Carraia built; in 1304 it collapses during the presentation of a mystery play
1220	Ponte Nuovo built as second permanent bridge across the Arno
1237	Ponte Rubaconte, named after Milanese podestà who rules Florence, is constructed
1237–50	Guelph-Ghibellini feud; power seesaws between the two factions for a generation, with the Guelphs eventually emerging triumphant
1248	First new city walls built since Roman times are begun as city's population tops 100,000
1252	Ponte Santa Trinita erected
1254	"Year of Victory": Guelphs extend hegemony over all of Tuscany
1254–1782	Inquisition maintains tribunal in Santa Croce
1260	Defeat of Florentine army at walls of Siena in battle of Montaperti; Ghibellines assume control of Florence for next seven years
1280	During era of reconciliation Guelphs, exiled in 1260, are permitted to return to city
1289	Freeing of the serfs
1293	Ordinamenti della Giustizia (Ordinances of Justice) enacted
1294–1303	Duomo (Santa Maria del Fiore) constructed
1299	Foundations of Palazzo Vecchio laid
1300	Papal jubilee brings representatives of twelve Western European powers to Florence
1303	Loggia on site of Or San Michele burns, but miraculous Madonna is saved
1312	Imperial army puts Florence to siege
1322	Sienese artisan casts huge bell for the Duomo tower
1332	Giotto appointed master builder of the Duomo
1333	Diastrous flood inundates Florence; third set of perimeter walls begun
1334	Giotto receives orders from Signoria, city's governing body, to increase Duomo "in size and richness"
1345	Flood-damaged Ponte Vecchio, dating from Roman times, extensively rebuilt on same site
1348	Bubonic plague—"Black Death"—wipes out two-thirds of the population of Florence
1349	Ringheria erected on Piazza della Signoria
1358	Tribunale de Mercatanzia established
1374–82	Loggia dei Lanzi constructed
1376	Or San Michele rebuilt as a church
1378	Revolt of the ciompi propels Salvestro de Medici to power
1382	Greater Guilds take over government of city
1403	Ghiberti wins famed competition to design the doors of the Baptistery
1405	Florence annexes Pisa
1418–20	Donatello executes Marzocco for Ringheria
1419–26	Ospedale degli Innocenti erected according to Brunelleschi's design
1429	Cosimo the Elder succeeds Giovanni as head of the increasingly powerful Medici clan
1434	Cosimo Pater Patriae becomes supreme ruler
1436	Brunelleschi's dome for Duomo consecrated at Feast of the Annunciation; Dominicans take over administration of San Marco
1439	General Council of the Catholic Church meets in Florence
1444	Cosimo founds Medici Library
1448	Piero de Medici commissions Chapel of the Crucifix for San Miniato
1452	Venice and Naples ally against Florence
1452–78	During epoch of unprecedented prosperity 30 palaces, 21 loggias, 138 gardens, 50 squares, and more than 800 villas are built in Florence
1464	Death of Cosimo
1466	Piero, Cosimo's successor, repels Venetian army

1469	Piero succeeded by Lorenzo, later known as "the Magnificent"
1478	Pazzi Conspiracy fails to unseat the Medici
1494	Piero de Medici obliged to entreat French army, encamped outside city walls, to spare Florence
1495	Donatello's *Judith,* made in 1460, moved to the Piazza della Signoria
1498	Savonarola burned at the stake in Piazza della Signoria seven years after first sermons in Duomo
1499	Campanile of San Miniato collapses
1503	Michelangelo and Leonardo da Vinci commissioned to produce frescoes for Salone dei Cinquencento in the Palazzo Vecchio
1504	Michelangelo's *David,* unveiled in Piazza della Signoria, provokes widespread public scorn
1512	Medici, briefly expelled from Florence in 1497, return to power
1519	Death of Lorenzo the Magnificent
1523	Cosimo I supercedes Signoria as ruler of city
1527	Machiavelli finishes *The Prince*
1532	Alessandro de Medici becomes new Duke of Florence
1534	Michelangelo quits Florence for Rome
1539	Cosimo I married to Eleanora of Toledo
1547	Mercato Nuovo opens
1552	Eleanora and two sons die of malaria at their villa on the outskirts of Florence
1553	Cosimo commissions Cellini's *Perseus* after the Medici are returned to power
1557	Cosimo resolves to rebuild Ponte Santa Trinita, destroyed by floods; work completed in 1569
1569	Recently named Grand Duke of Tuscany, Cosimo lures French expert to city to teach art of mosaic
1574	Death of Cosimo; Francesco succeeds, has secret underground passage built from his residence, Pitti Palace, to home of mistress on Via Maggio
1575	Ammannati's *Fountain of Neptune* completed
1578	Francesco marries Bianca Cappello on death of his wife, Joanna
1583	Giambologna's *Rape of a Sabine* added to the Loggia
1586	Duomo façade torn down; many statues by Pisano and Donatello lost
1609	Cosimo II succeeds Ferdinando
1628	Ferdinando II, successor to Cosimo II in 1620, deals bravely with outbreaks of the plague
1633	Pope summons Galileo to Rome
1636	Inquisition at height; suspected heretics

	burned at the stake in piazza in front of Santa Croce
1638	Milton visits Galileo, now under house arrest, in Torre del Galileo outside Florence
1642	Death of Galileo
1657	Accademia del Cimento founded
1670–1723	Reign of Cosimo III; Medici and their city begin long, slow decline in importance
1711	Pianoforte invented in Florence by Bartolommeo Cristofori
1736	Peace of Vienna awards Tuscany to Francis, Duke of Lorraine
1773	Society of Jesus dissolved
1796	Napoleon conquers most of northern Italy
1799	French driven out of Tuscany by Russian general Suvarov, only to return a year later after Napoleon's great victory at Marengo
1805	All Italy (except Sicily and Sardinia) goes to Napoleon after Battle of Austerlitz
1812	Invading French army destroys Ringheria; Napoleon appropriates treasures of Laurentian Library
1815	Congress of Vienna; Ferdinand III returns
1837	William Wordsworth visits Florence, sits on "Dante's seat" near the Duomo
1846	Robert and Elizabeth Barrett Browning settle in Florence, where she dies in 1861
1848–59	Provisional Government uses Palazzo Vecchio as an assembly hall
1859	Grand Duke abdicates
1871–87	Neo-Gothic façade added to Duomo
1894	Botticelli's *Pallas Subduing the Centaur,* painted in late 1500s to commemorate the Medici triumph in the Pazzi Conspiracy, found in Pitti Palace
1865–71	Florence briefly succeeds Turin as capital of united Italy
1868	Dostoyevsky, visiting Florence, writes *The Idiot*
1878	Tchaikovsky stays on Via San Leonardo
1904	Professor Elia Volpe buys Palazzo Davanzati and restores it before giving it to city
1932	Pier Luigi Nervi designs Stadio Communale
1944	Retreating Germans blow all bridges over the Arno
1958	Ponte Trinita rebuilt, perfect in every detail
1961	Elizabeth II pays a state visit to Florence
1966	Worst flood since 1333 sweeps through Florence; incalculable damage done to Ponte Vecchio, Duomo, Baptistery and other major buildings; private homes, art works, manuscripts also destroyed; major international effort mounted to salvage and restore these damaged masterpieces

163

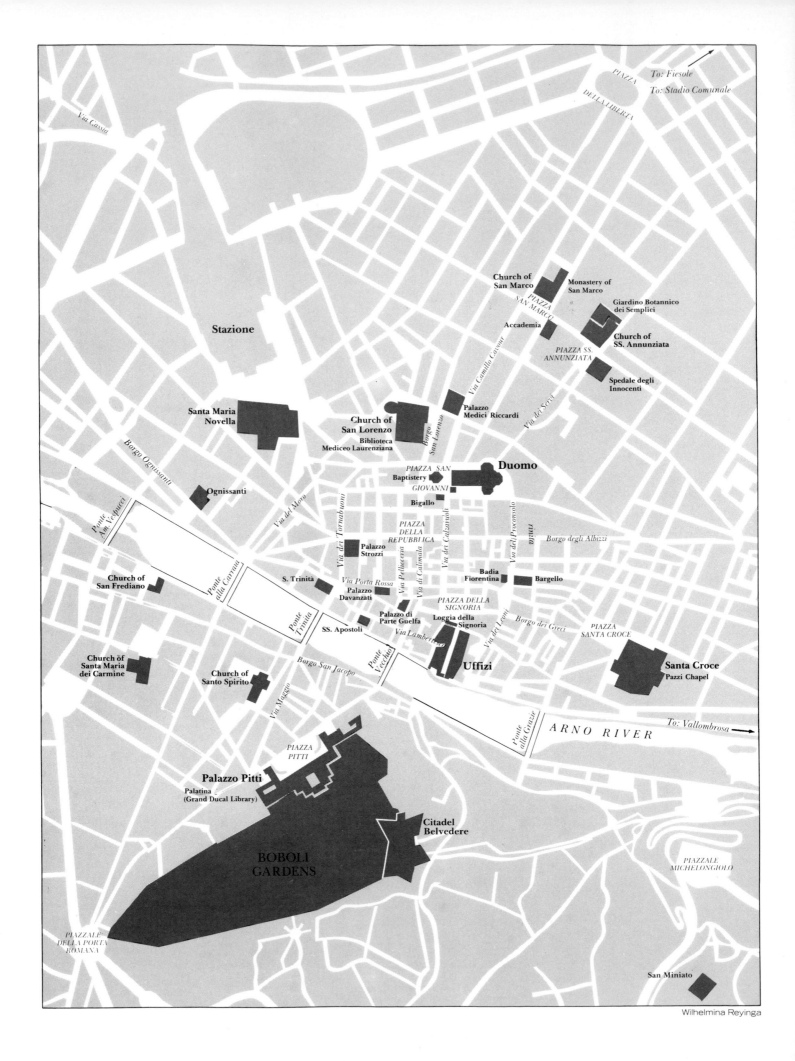

Via Cassia

To: Fiesole
To: Stadio Comunale

PIAZZA DELLA LIBERTÀ

Stazione

Church of San Marco
Monastery of San Marco
PIAZZA SAN MARCO
Accademia
Giardino Botannico dei Semplici
Church of SS. Annunziata
PIAZZA SS. ANNUNZIATA
Spedale degli Innocenti

Santa Maria Novella

Church of San Lorenzo
Biblioteca Mediceo Laurenziana

Palazzo Medici Riccardi

Borgo San Lorenzo

Via Camillo Cavour

Via dei Servi

Borgo Ognissanti

Ognissanti

Ponte Am. Vespucci

PIAZZA SAN GIOVANNI
Baptistery

Duomo

Bigallo

Via del Moro

Via dei Tornabuoni

PIAZZA DELLA REPUBBLICA

Palazzo Strozzi

Via Calzaioli

Via Pellicceria

Via Calzaioli

Via dell'Proconsolo

Borgo degli Albizzi

Church of San Frediano

Ponte alla Carraia

S. Trinità

Via Porta Rossa

Palazzo Davanzati

Badia Fiorentina

Bargello

Church of Santa Maria dei Carmine

Ponte Trinita

SS. Apostoli

Palazzo di Parte Guelfa

PIAZZA DELLA SIGNORIA

Loggia della Signoria

Via dei Leoni

Borgo dei Greci

PIAZZA SANTA CROCE

Church of Santo Spirito

Borgo San Jacopo

Ponte Vecchio

Via Lambertesca

Uffizi

Santa Croce
Pazzi Chapel

Via Maggio

Ponte alla Grazie

ARNO RIVER

To: Vallombrosa

PIAZZA PITTI

Palazzo Pitti
Palatina (Grand Ducal Library)

Citadel Belvedere

PIAZZALE MICHELONGIOLO

BOBOLI GARDENS

PIAZZALE DELLA PORTA ROMANA

San Miniato

Wilhelmina Reyinga

Guide to Florence

A visitor, by definition, has something less than a lifetime to spend exploring the manifold delights of Florence—its art and architecture, its palaces and piazzas, its galleries and gardens, its tapestries and frescoes, its heroic public statuary and its delicate enamels and goldwork. In the days of the Grand Tour, that leisurely sojourn on the Continent which put the final burnish on a English gentleman's education, it was not uncommon for a young peer and his party to stop for weeks or even months in the cradle of the Renaissance. Others—expatriate aesthetes, disenfranchised wanderers, refugees from various forms of oppression, political, moral and sexual—were to settle more or less permanently in Florence. The poets Robert and Elizabeth Barrett Browning, together the lexus of literary and social Florence during the middle decades of the last century, lived for years in the magnificent Casa Guidi on Via Maggio and came to know their adopted city far better than most natives.

Few modern visitors to the city of Dante and Boccaccio, Michelangelo and Donatello, Fra Angelico and Fra Filippo Lippi, Bramante and Brunelleschi, Giotto and Ghiberti have the luxury of time. The leisurely tour, the lengthy stay are things of the past—nineteenth-century luxuries that faded with that century. The modern visitor's acquaintance with Florence is likely to be a fleeting one—two days, three; ten at the most—but that does not mean it cannot be a happy and rewarding acquaintance.

It is, by common consent, impossible to see all there is to see in Florence in a week, a month, a year—even, some would insist, in an entire lifetime. This does not mean that a visitor cannot get a solid sense of what the city is like in a very few days, however, especially if he confines his sightseeing to a fairly restricted area each day, one that can be covered on foot.

If you have but a single day in Florence, spend it in the Piazza del Duomo. The great cathedral of Santa Maria del Fiore, as the **Duomo** is officially known, is one of the largest cathedrals in Christendom, and after only St. Peter's in Rome, the most magnificently decorated. Begun in 1296 and consecrated in 1436, this huge, cloverleaf-shaped structure of multicolored marble is surmounted by a vast dome, 365 feet in height, that took fourteen years to complete. Brunelleschi's soaring dome, with its red tile cupola and gleaming white marble ribs, is visible from far outside the city. Its inner surfaces are covered with a mammoth fresco of the Last Judgment by Vasari and Zuccari, and the whole is lit by stained glass windows wrought from cartoons prepared by Ghiberti, Donatello, Paolo Uccello, and others. The great octagonal chancel that lies directly beneath the dome was the site, in 1478, of the ill-fated Pazzi Conspiracy, which sought to oust the Medici from power and succeeded only in killing one of their number. The manifold treasures of the Duomo include Ghiberti's sarcophagus for St. Zenobius, the first bishop of Florence, and the deeply affecting *Pietà* that Michelangelo left unfinished at his death.

Adjacent to the southwest corner of the Duomo is the **Campanile** designed by Giotto in 1334 and completed some sixty years after his death in 1336. Although Gothic in style, this slim tower, which rises 269 feet above the Piazza del Duomo, is Classical in spirit. Its elegant lines are also sheathed in polychrome marble, and its base is inset with bas-reliefs, copies of original designs by Andrea Pisano and Luca della Robbia.

The octagonal **Baptistery**, which stands just west of the Duomo, is one of the oldest buildings in Florence—recollected by Dante, who called the place where he was baptised "my lovely San Giovanni." Romanesque in design and dating from the eleventh century, the Baptistery merits consideration on purely architectural terms, but its fabled bronze doors—on the north, south, and east sides of the building—so overshadow the structure itself that few casual visitors remark on the building as a whole. Of the doors, the north is the most famous, its design the end-product of a now-legendary competition between Brunelleschi and Lorenzo Ghiberti. Ghiberti, winner of that contest, was to design the east door as well—and when finished this portal was to earn the accolade "Gate to Paradise" from Michelangelo himself. The south door, the work of Andrea Pisano, is covered with scenes from the life of John the Baptist.

If you have but a single nice day in Florence, spend it outdoors—in the **Piazza della Signoria** and along the banks of the Arno. The Piazza, an irregular polygon bordered by the Palazzo Vec-

chio, the Loggia della Signoria, and the Uffizi Museum, was the political heart of the Medici empire, and the civic and cultural center of the High Renaissance. The dominant structure on the Piazza is the **Palazzo Vecchio**, or Old Palace. As much fortress as palace, this imposing Gothic edifice, with its crenelated battlements and parapet walks, recalls a time when the civic stability of Florence was threatened as much by enemies within as enemies without. The men who built the Palazzo Vecchio between 1299 and 1314 feared factionalism among Florentines more than the prospect of a foreign army's laying siege to the city, and they constructed their citadel to withstand both kinds of onslaught. The rude exterior of the Palazzo Vecchio, which is attributed to Arnolfo di Cambio, designer of the Duomo, belies its elegant interior, extensively restored by Michelozzo in 1453 and further embellished a century later. On the first floor of the Palazzo is the cavernous Sala dei Cinquecento, resplendent with fresoces by Giorgio Vasari depicting episodes from Florentine history. A niche in one wall holds Michelangelo's *Victory*, probably carved for the tomb of Pope Julius II. Upstairs are the so-called Priors' Apartments, the most sumptuous of which is the Sala dei Gigli, or Hall of the Lilies—the lily being the symbol of Florence. This huge audience chamber has a coffered ceiling by Giuliano da Maiano and frescoes by Ghirlandaio.

On the rough paving stones in front of the Palazzo Vecchio stand three sculptures of great consequence: Donatello's *Marzocco*, a representation of the guardian lion that represents Florence in medieval heraldry; the same sculptor's *Judith with the Head of Holofernes*, a monumental bronze as graphic as it is arresting; and a copy of Michelangelo's world-famous *David*. Immediately adjacent is the **Loggia della Signoria**, constructed in the late 1300s as an assembly hall for the *lanzi*, or foot-soldiers, who served Cosimo the Younger, Duke of Tuscany. As a result, it is frequently referred to as the Loggia dei Lanzi. Its covered arcade functions today as one of the city's foremost sculpture galleries. Among its Renaissance treasures are Giovanni da Bologna's *Hercules* and his *Rape of a Sabine*. Its undisputed masterpiece, however, is Benvenuto Cellini's *Perseus*, executed between 1545 and 1553.

Between the Palazzo Vecchio and the Loggia della Signoria, at the southernmost point of the Piazza della Signoria, lies the entrance to the **Galleria degli Uffizi**. The great museum, once the offices of the mighty Medici family's commercial empire, rises on either side of this gallery, and a prospect of the Arno is framed by the colonnade at the gallery's far end. A closed walkway, the so-called Vasari Corridor, connects the Uffizi with the vast Pitti Palace on the south bank of the Arno, but in clement weather the visitor will want to opt for the street, not the corridor, as a means of reaching the Pitti Palace and its gardens.

Vasari's mile-long corridor forms the topmost story of **Ponte Vecchio**, so named because it is the oldest of Florence's Arno bridges. Spans of one sort or another have stood on this site since Roman times, but the present bridge dates from the fourteenth century, when the disastrous flood of 1333 swept away all traces of its predecessors. An unusual feature of the Ponte Vecchio is its shops and stalls, which line both sides of the covered walkway that runs down the center of the bridge and are cantilevered out over the Arno itself. Originally these shops were rented to butchers, but in the sixteenth century, at the behest of Cosimo I, they were leased to goldsmiths—a tradition that persists to this day.

The most monumental of Florentine palaces, the **Pitti Palace**, lies at the nether end of the Vasari Corridor. Its central section, three stories of rusticated stone and massive arches, is the handiwork of Brunelleschi; the flanking wings, although similar in style, are eighteenth-century additions. Of particular interest to the visitor are the Royal Apartments and the Palantine Gallery, with its superb collection of Titians and Raphaels. Both are found on the palace's first floor.

South and west of the Pitti Palace are the famed **Boboli Gardens**, once a private reserve of the Medici and now Florence's largest public park. The gardens, which form a rough triangle, are demarcated by Buontalenti's Grotto at the northern apex, the Porta della Romana

at the southwest corner, and the Citadel Belvedere at the southeast corner. The star-shaped citadel affords an unparalleled view of the city and its surrounding hills, an inspiration to painters, poets, and other visitors through the ages. Of special interest in the gardens is the Viottolone, an avenue of cypresses and pines that runs from the amphitheatre, on the gardens' northern edge, to the Piazzale dell' Isolotto, a reflecting pool containing an artificial island and a fountain by Giovanni da Bologna. The gardens are little changed today from the original park laid out by Tribolo in the 1550s and augmented over the next several decades by Ammannati and Buontalenti.

Having spent a full day outdoors, you will want to spend much of another day, a day when the skies are lowering and a fine rain is falling over Florence, indoors. Begin with the vast **Uffizi Museum**, the subject of another Newsweek Book (see Selected Bibliography, page 168). Housed in a Renaissance palace designed by Vasari in the mid-sixteenth century, its collections are among the world's finest. Of particular interest are the Flemish tapestries and classical statuary in the galleries, the masterworks by Cimabue, Giotto, and Duccio on the first floor, and the incomparable Botticelli Room, which contains his *Birth of Venus* and *Primavera*. On the second floor are galleries devoted to works by Raphael, Michelangelo, Andrea del Sarto, and other giants of the Cinquecento.

North of the Uffizi along the Via del Proconsolo stands the imposing bulk of the **Bargello**, once headquarters of the city's constabulary and now a major museum, as famous for its beautiful courtyard and splendid staircases as for its collections of enamels, ivories and jewels. One entire room on the ground floor is given over to the works of Michelangelo and his sixteenth-century contemporaries. These include, in addition to Michelangelo's *Bacchus*, a *David* and *St. George* by Donatello and yet another *David*, this one by Verrocchio. Benvenuto Cellini's familiar bust of Cosimo I is here, as is Michelangelo's tondo, *Madonna and Child*, and other Madonnas in glazed terracotta by those masters of the form Luca and Andrea della Robbia.

The church and cloisters of **Santa Croce**, often referred to as the Westminister Abbey of Florence, are to be found several blocks east of the Bargello, fronting on a square that bears the same name. Begun in 1294 by the Franciscan Order and finished some sixty years later, Santa Croce is remarkable for its treasures as well as its tombs. The latter include the crypts of Lorenzo Ghiberti, Michelangelo, and Galileo, among many others. The former include chancel frescoes by Giotto and Agnolo Gaddi; a Crucifix by Donatello in the north transept and another, equally famous, by Cimabue in the cloisters; and the Pazzi Chapel, one of Brunelleschi's supreme efforts; embellished with terracottas from the della

Robbia workshops. Only slightly less magnificent are the Baroncelli and Rinuccini chapels, and the Medici Chapel created in 1434 by Michelozzo.

If your visit to Florence lasts less than a lifetime but more than three days, visit the great church of **Santa Maria Novella**, erected by the Dominicans in the thirteenth and fourteenth centuries. With its green and white marble façade, its frescoes by Masaccio and Orcagna, and its Giotto Crucifix, it is worth a day in itself. So, for that matter, is the Galleria dell'Accademia, or **Academy Gallery**, where Michelangelo's *Four Slaves*, unfinished at the sculptor's death and intended for the tomb of Pope Julius II, are to be found alongside the original *David*, perhaps the most famous work in all of sculpture and certainly the most famous in Florence. Within walking distance of the Accademia is **San Lorenzo**, a Renaissance church from Brunelleschi's hand that contains the renowned Laurentian Library, a collection of 10,000 manuscripts housed in a great chamber designed by Michelangelo and reached by a majestic staircase executed by Ammannati after Michelangelo's designs. Nearby can be found the **Palazzo Medici-Riccardi**, built in 1444 by Michelozzo for Cosimo the Elder and inhabited by family members until 1540.

What you have seen, when you have completed this abbreviated tour, is but a tiny fraction of Florence's treasures. Enough to give you a sense of what you have missed; enough to lure you back to explore the rest.

Selected Bibliography

Bonechi, Edoardo. *Florence: A Complete Guide for Visiting the City.* Bonechi Guides-Mercurio Series, 1972.

Borsook, Eve. *The Companion Guide to Florence.* New York: Harper and Row, 1966.

Chiarelli, Renzo. *San Lorenzo and the Medici Chapels.* International Publications Serivce, 1971.

Hurlimann, Martin and Harold Acton. *Florence.* New York: Viking Press, 1961.

Hutton, Edward. *Florence.* New York: David McKay, 1952.

McCarthy, Mary. *Stones of Florence.* New York: Harcourt, Brace, 1976.

Machiavelli, Niccolo. *History of Florence.* New York: Harper and Row, 1960.

Martinelli, Giuseppi, ed. *The World of Renaissance Florence.* New York: Putnam's, 1968.

Molajoli, Bruno. *Florence.* New York: Holt, Rinehart and Winston, 1972.

Taylor, Kathrine Kressman. *Diary of Florence in Flood.* New York: Simon and Schuster, 1967.

Uffizi Museum. New York: Newsweek Books, 1968.

Acknowledgements and Picture Credits

The modern photographs of Florence are the work of Nicolas Sapieha. The title or description of the other illustrations appears after the page number (boldface), followed by its location. The following abbreviations are used:

(NS) — Nicolas Sapieha
(S) — Scala—Editorial Photo Archives

The Editors are particularly grateful to Laura Lane at American Heritage Publishing Company in New York and to Susanna Rausch and Virginia Prina at Gruppo Editoriale Fabbri in Milan. In addition they would like to thank Dr. Maria Todorov of the Palazzo Davanzati; Richard Fremantle; Maria Teresa Train of Scala Books; Cristina Capua; Alessandra Marchi of Centro Di; and Laboratorio Center Chrome, Florence.

ENDPAPERS Detail from the Campanile, Duomo. (NS) HALF-TITLE Symbol of Florence by Jay J. Smith TITLEPAGE Dickens' view of the Arno. (NS) **9** Donatello, *Marzocco* Bargello (Fabbri) **10**(NS) **12–13** Map of Florence, 1490. Museum of Florence (S)

CHAPTER I **14** Leonardo da Vinci, *Lily.* Windsor Castle, By Gracious Permission of Her Majesty the Queen **16–19** (NS) **20–21** (Alinari) **23–27** (NS)

CHAPTER II **29** Lorenzo Ghiberti, Baptistery door. (Alinari) **30–31** (NS) **32** Sandro Botticelli, *Three Miracles of Saint Zenobius.* Metropolitan Museum Art **33–37** (NS) **39** Pavement detail from San Miniato. (Alinari) **40–45** (NS)

CHAPTER III **47** Emblem of Florence, Palazzo Ferroni. (Alinari) **48–51** (NS) **53** Emblem of the Wool-Makers Guild. Museo dell'Opera del Duomo (Courtesy American Heritage Publishing Company) **54–55** (NS) **57** Cimabue, *Madonna Enthroned.* Uffizi (S) **58–63** (NS) **64–65** Paolo Uccello, *Battle of San Romano.* Louvre (S)

CHAPTER IV **67** (NS) **69** Dante, *Divine Comedy.* Bibliothéque Nationale, Paris Ms. Italian Coc. **74** fol lv 71 top right Castagno, *Petrarch.* Convent of Sant'Apollonia top left *Boccaccio,* Bibliothéque Nationale, Paris Codex **38** bottom da Ponte, *Dante.* Biblioteca Ricardiana, Florence Ms. 1040 fol 1 **72** Bellotto, *Piazza della Signoria, Florence. Budapest Museum* (S) **74–79** (NS)

CHAPTER V **81** Museo degli Argenti (NS) **82** Bernardo Sgrillius, *S. Maria del Fiore,* New York Public Library **82–85** (NS) **86–87** Benozzo Gozzoli, *Procession of the Magi.* Palazzo, Medici, Florence (S) **89** Fra Angelico and Fra Filippo Lippi, *Adoration of the Magi.* National Gallery of Art, Kress Collection **90** Donatello, *David.* Museo Nazionale, Florence **92** Villa Medici, Cafaggiolo, 16th century. Photo R. Soprintendenza, Florence **93** Andrea del Verrocchio, *Lorenzo de Medici.* National Gallery of Art, Washington **95** *Lorenzo and Giuliano de Medici,* the Pazzi Conspiracy, 1478. National Gallery of Art, Kress Collection **97** Sandro Botticelli, *Pallas Subduing the Centaur.* Uffizi, Florence (S) **98–99** Michelangelo, *Studies.* All: British Museum **101** Fra Bartolommeo, *Girolamo Savonarola.* S. Marco, Florence (S) **102–103** Portraits of Florentines, 15–16th centuries. From left, by artist: Botticelli, Ghirlandaio, Lippi, Biagio d'Antonio, da Vinci. All: National Gallery of Art, Washington **104–105** (NS)

CHAPTER VI **107** Cellini, *Cosimo de Medici.* Museo Nazionale, Florence **108** right Agnolo Bronzino, *Cosimo I de Medici.* Uffizi (Fabbri) left Agnolo Bronzino, *Eleonora de Toledo.* National Gallery of Art, Washington **109–115** (NS) **116–117** Both-Medici Chapel, Florence. (S) **118** Design for a clock by Galileo. Biblioteca Nazionale, Florence. Ms. Galileano 85–c–50 **119** Ottavio Leoni, *Galileo.* Biblioteca Nazionale, Florence **120–23** (NS)

CHAPTER VII **125–128** (NS) **129** Wide World **130–31** (NS) **132–33** All: Wide World **134–135** (NS)

FLORENCE IN LITERATURE All: (NS)

REFERENCE **164** Map of Florence Wilhelmina Reyinga

Index